STRAIGHT TWIGS
a KidGrower's GuideBook

Foreword by Elizabeth Bolton

With articles by—
   Jenny Lakey
   Vicki Jacobsen
   Ryan J. Spickard
   Sonja Ann McGucken
   Andrea Crain
   Heather Shipe

Illustrators—
   Tanya Crenshaw
   Joey Novak

Susan Henry

Alpha Books
Rickreall, Oregon

Library of Congress Catalog Catalog Card Number: 92-70567
ISBN 0-943149-12-6
Alpha Books, Box 13, Rickreall, Oregon 97371
Manufactured in the United States of America

To my children's children—
Stephanie, Samantha
Susan, James
Arie,
who have given a new meaning
to everything

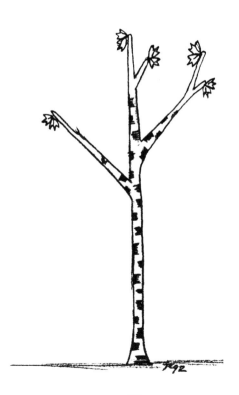

Foreword

When Birmingham Elementary School opened in Wylie, Texas in 1987, some people considered it to be nothing more than a holding ground for kids scheduled to be losers. It was the school which should have failed.

But the kids at Birmingham were winners right off the mark. "Every Kid Is A Top Kid" isn't just a slogan there — it's a policy: Here's-your-prophecy-Now-go-fulfill-it. These kids who were scheduled to be losers now take top awards in all state assessments.

This I believe is equally important: The whole town is involved with this school. Parents, banks, businesses; even the historical society; and the local TV, radio, and newspaper, who proclaim and applaud. Yes, they feed kids breakfast; yes, they educate parents; yes, they start with preschools and child care providers.

I know Birmingham because I had a hand in composing the school's nomination for a National Blue Ribbon Schools award. I am also aware of the pheonomenal, national-attention success of Madison Middle School, West Seattle, and Hollibrook Elementary School, Houston, two schools accepted into Stanford University's prestigous and acclaimed Accelerated Schools Project.

Madison strives to do as much for all students as other schools do only for those labeled "Gifted and Talented." At Madison, part of the same curriculum used for the honors section is being taught to at-risk students. And it's working. And like Birmingham, Madison gets parents and the whole community *involved*. These towns are proud of their schools. is a big talking poing — people move to Wylie because of the school. This, I think, is a critical factor in a school's success, and in a child's.

If you looked at the statistics for Hollibrook Elementary School, Houston, you'd be sure this, too, was a school that should fail to provide a quality education. Of its 1,000 students, 97% are eligible for free or reduced lunches, and 84% come to school with limited or no English.

But Hollibrook, like Birmingham and Madison, doesn't put the word Failure in its program. Hollibrook's theme is something like You Can Do It, Kid! You Are Somebody!

Does it work? Well, these thousand youngsters — kids whom "society" (who and whatever that is) assigned to failure — picked up 2 grade levels in two years. After only 2 1/2 years into the project, most of Hollibrook's students score at or near grade level in those all-important tests.

I am strongly reminded of these schools as I read Straight Twigs: a KidGrower's GuideBook. I have seen that the propositions Susan Henry sets forth are true: That adults must provide kids with exposure, experience, and opportunitiy to grow and do and be; that kids are capable of taking these experiences and running farther with them than they or we realize; that nutrition and family may be even more important than education in the making of a person.

Through my own first-hand experiences, I can validate Henry's views that fostering creativity and developing a consuming interest in something are the means to com-pleting the person. I saw this work with kids, when, for 23 years, I was director of a children's camp, Sherwood Forest, where I wrote and staged plays. I've observed it work for adults as well, in the acting workshops and poetry classes I've taught over the years at Marylhurst College and other sites. In fact, in her chapters, "Non-Achievers" and "SOAR!", Henry makes a great case for my Acting Workshop texts for high schoolers and adults.

It is one of those coincidences of life that Sherwood Forest was in Nahcotta, Washington . . . only a few miles from Susan's hometown. In fact, I first arrived at Sherwood Forest only a short time after Susan's chemistry experiment caused the evacuation of Ilwaco High School. She tells you about that in here, too.

ELIZABETH BOLTON
Portland, Oregon

STRAIGHT TWIGS
—a KidGrower's GuideBook

Introduction

Bending the twig. That has long been our colloquialism for raising children, for shaping and forming their values and behavior. In the plant kingdom, tiny young saplings are shaped by winds and rocks and browsers and by neighbors which cast too much shade or crowd too close. During their first season or two of growth, young saplings are permanently bent and shaped according to their environment.

Trees that grow gnarls and knots and picturesque contortions are things of beauty to artists and photographers; but crooked and bent is not a good way to form children. Better than *bent* twigs, it seems to me, is *straight* twigs.

Guiding kids is the most awesome job there is. Anyone who works with children realizes that; and anyone who doesn't is not taking his charge seriously enough. Yet one can be a parent with no prerequisites, no training, and no credential — while the person who cuts your hair must pass an exam and get a license.

Generally people young enough to have little kids are too inexperienced to know what to do with them. People who are mellowed-out and experienced don't have the stamina to keep up with little guys, and certainly not with teenagers. Perhaps this ironic plan proves God has a sense of humor; or perhaps She was challenging us to work it out. Obviously, Her final choice was inexperience with energy and adaptability, over wisdom with arthritis and fatigue.

For decades I've read advice columns and books on How To Handle Children. The problem is, the answers are generic, and my kids are not generic. And the answers keep changing. By the time my third child was born, Dr. Spock had changed his mind about what I should have done with the first. There must be some more enduring answers.

Don't believe yourself not wise enough to derive your own answers. If babes were born only to the wise enough and deserving enough, there would have been no children after Cain and Abel.

During my years as an educator and a journalist, I've met a lot of people, seen a lot of stories — a *lot* of stories: nothing in this book is made up, nothing is embellished; nothing needed to be. While stage and costume change across time, the basic qualities of kids do not. Infants still turn over before they walk, and teenagers still can't wait to get out of the house. And, a woman of 77 told me, "My folks were horrified at the awful music I liked in 1926."

Not all the analyses and conclusions in this book are wholly, solely my own. Over the years I have drawn from mentors of great horsepower: Jane and Bill and a sprinkle of others; a few journalists, especially Goodman and Royko; my kids (by their mid-twenties their dad and I got over not knowing anything); and, mostly, Bob. And from the persons Bob and I ask when we can't make up our minds — our little granddaughters.

Other voices come from the cameo contributors to this book, whose bylines appear on their articles; from experts in their various fields, whose comments and advice are attributed; and from countless individuals across America who answered my questions. Their contributions add depth and dimension, for they do not necessarily agree with my viewpoints, nor was it required that they do.

When your children are small, every day is a critical point in time for *you.* From early schoolhood on, every question, dilemma, and event is the biggest deal of a lifetime for *them;* at every snag, they are certain they'll just die.

From about age 10 onward, kids' most important influences are their friends, their heroes (mostly athletes and entertainers), and whatever is In so they can belong to it. The plant is formed. That those critical years are so soon over makes some parents scared — and some, relieved.

There will come a time that you will be able to step away from the moment-by-moment and see a long, expansive, richly textured, multiple layered mural, a continuum of life and lives, all woven together. If you look closely at your children, you can see your own childhood; and in your childhood, you can see your grandchildren as adults.

1

Imprints and Influences

The roots of the tree

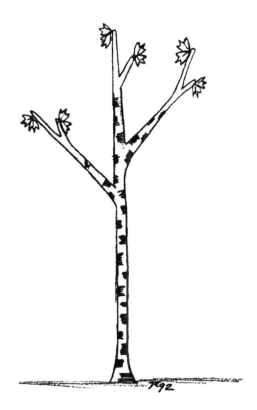

Cover artist Tanya Crenshaw is a student at South Salem High School, Salem, Oregon. Her themes are reprised at the beginning of each section of this book.

1

Making chances

His name was Paul Malcolm Borthton The Third, which didn't fit him so they called him Boot, which did. Her name was Wynodette and they called her Wynne, which fit her precisely. Boot and Wynne arrived in Alaska in the mid-sixties, when the Bureau of Indian Affairs operated the schools in Native villages. That was what the Borthtons came to do, to teach.

She said she didn't bring any particular talents or skills. "I just want to be a good teacher," she said. Boot didn't care much about the schoolwork part; he intended to introduce sports to the Eskimos and teach them to be athletes.

They met those goals, and more.

Boot began his agenda quietly. Well, quietly for him. Of all the BIA teachers in all the villages, he was the most bombastic personality of two decades. First, as part of his PE program and then, gradually introducing it as an after-school activity, Boot began training his upper grade boys to wrestle. Parents approved; the sport gained momentum.

Suddenly, it turned out that most of the male teachers in bush Alaska had been frustrated jocks all along, and coach types sprung up from the floorboards. Within three or four years the Yukon-Kuskokwim BIA schools had a full-fledged interscholastic elementary wrestling program, complete with trained, certified officials, coaches, and tournaments.

But to Boot, one sport did not a program equal. So he and his teaching-coaching colleagues instituted basketball in the village schools. After that, after the Native kids discovered they possessed interests and abilities never before tapped, volleyball and cross-country skiing and running were introduced.

If athletics is the axiom, then cheerleading is its correlary. "I'm not sure I can pull this off," Wynne told friends. She did, magnificently. It was she who introduced cheerleading to the Yukon-Kuskokwim Delta. Not the Yay-Team spin-and-jump of the forties and fifties, but the athletic, aerobic choreography of today, played out to taped pop tunes of the time.

"Not the way I remember cheerleading," huffed the older teachers; but it caught on. Grade schoolers in remote Eskimo villages of Alaska had mastered the "new cheerleading" style before was "In" in the Lower 48. Cheerleading grew along with athletics, and the schools sponsored clinics to train the youngsters, and trophy competitions to reward them.

While Boot had no patience with kids who couldn't shine in sports, Wynne did. So, with only her high school flute and a twenty-dollar guitar as musical background, she instituted a band in her grade school. "If you have enthusiasm, you can make people think you have talent," she once said cheerfully.

Wynne led the school kids, the villagers, and teachers throughout Western Alaska to another realization: The Yup'ik Eskimo youngster possessed an inate musical skill. "You hand an Eskimo kid a horn and it plays itself," BIA education specialist Cal Lundy once said. And Wynne said, "The kids would never have realized this skill if we had not given them the chance to find out."

The musical movement grew along the Kuskokwim River and the lower Yukon; but Wynne's band was the first, and always, it was the best among the thirty little schools in the region. Everywhere she went, Wynne took her guitar, even to athletic events. Soon the Native kids knew all the old standby camp songs and folk tunes and were that many steps closer to understanding the Western culture which was being woven into their own.

People who liked Boot — they were legion — said he was merely gruff; others called him crude. Though claiming to be of Old Boston heritage, he speech and manner were more street-Brooklyn. He was the only teacher I ever knew who could call his students *little fahts* and have the parents like it.

The ever ready outdoorsman kept his "geah box" in the center of the miniature living room of their government quarters. It was a rustic home-made wooden box the size of a small coffin, and it held tools, tarps, trail rations, and firearms. Wynne walked around it, not complaining, even when Boot cleaned and cured a sealskin in the living room, or left mounds of sawdust on the carpet.

They remained for a decade and a half, then returned to New England to settle in a town that ranks about ten-thousandth in Name Familiarity Of U.S. Cities. Wynne said she was not going to teach again, but the wolf panted and she was the first to return to the classroom.

Boot ricochetted from job to job — day camp, juvenile home, law enforcement. It was teeth-grinding difficult for him, not being the instigator, innovator, the head man. After eight years, Boot once again was teaching, not principal as he once was, but coaching, which he preferred anyway.

Years later Wynne said of her Alaska experience, "It gave me the chance to stretch more and achieve more than I ever dreamed I could."

> "Kids can stretch and reach, more than anyone thinks. But only if we create opportunities for them so they can." — *Wynne Borthton*

Joey Novak's parents discovered his artistic talent, then guided and encouraged him as he developed it. Before he reached teen age, he was selling his sketches and winning awards. Nobody refers to him as "that severely developmentally delayed boy"; he is known as "that incredible artist."

2

Show them the door

"This is association," I told Sophomore English. "I say something, you say the first word that comes to mind. . . .
"Door." . . . "*Knock.*"
"Knocks." . . . "*Opportunity.*"
"Seize — ". . . "*Opportunity.*"
"Blow — ". . . "*Chance.*"

Somehow. Opportunity has come to be associated with a door. Opportunity knocks. We open the door to it. We step through the Doorway of it. We grab it . . . or blow it.

Jargoneers variously call it Exposure, Experience, Exploring, Experimenting or The Chance To Try; but by whatever name, Opportunity means Finding Out What's There And Doing Something About It. Without finding the opportunity, then grabbing it, nobody can use his talents, aptitudes, or potentials; he won't even know he has them. If Ray Charles had never touched a piano, if Mark Twain were never given a pen, nor Michael Jordan a basketball . . . had they not worked, concentrated, and practiced . . .

Education texts call seeing, doing, and finding out about things, a *background of experience*. That's edu-gab for "stuff you know about."

When kids are messing around, messing up, and trying out — like collecting ants, taking the vacuum cleaner apart, and melting crayons on the stove — the trendword is *exploring*.

For a number of years Bob and I lived and taught in remote areas of Alaska, where no roads connected village to village, where there were no trees, gardens, flowers, no farms or livestock; no restaurants (hamburgers were not in the culture), no bakeries (nor doughnuts); no parks, swings, teeters; where the only musical instruments were the pump-organs in the church and an occasional guitar. What do you suppose children grew up knowing about, and what talents do you think got tapped?

Thanks to people like Boot and Wynne, various tools of doing were introduced, year by year, one or two at a time. Wrestling mats and basketballs; acrylics and oils and potter's wheels; cookware, computers, clarinets, calculators and student-run school stores. It turned out that even in this setting which Westerners call barren, Alaska Native youngsters have inside them incredible aptitudes for drawing, athletics, and music; for creative cooking, computer programming, entrepreneurship — all the talents and knacks that are common to people everywhere.

There is no reason to doubt that all these aptitudes have been present, dormant, in the Eskimo people since time immemorial; yet as far as I know no Eskimo has become a welterweight champ nor a world-class saxophonist, and the reason ought to be obvious. Between the sixties and the eighties the kids were taken to door after door, and one after the other, they stepped through.

Ted and Jan Novak live across the creek that borders our farm. (We met them when our cattle jumped fence, forded the creek, and discovered the Novaks' corn patch. We settled up.) When their son Joey was yet a toddler, say the Novaks, "we became aware of what many people consider 'limitations'," and he spent his school years in special classes. Ted and Jan also became aware of Joey's special talents: "He has been blessed with exceptional visual memory and perception of intricate details," and a rare artistic ability to set his visions to paper.

Joey's parents supplied him with drawing paper and pens, and they took him on tours of the countryside, allowing him to examine buildings, bridges, and boats, giving him time, space, and equipment to draw them, and the encouragement to persevere. Lacking fine muscle control, the youngster learned to control his pen by drawing with both hands locked together, one atop the other.

Now Joey Novak is an established artist — he has received rave reviews, awards, and commissions — with a business of his own. "Line Upon Line" they call it, inspired by the words of Isaiah 28:13: ". . . precept upon precept, line upon line, here a little, there a little . . ." His works, an extensive output of intricate, detailed sketches, are available as 8-by-10 and 4 by 6 lithographs and notecards, which Line Upon Line markets assertively. I don't hear Joey Novak referred to as "that severely retarded boy"; I hear of him as "that incredible savant, whose parents found his gift."

Adults and older youngsters, from middle grades onward, can empower themselves by finding and making their own opportunities, and can exert the effort to discover and develop their own skills — not only can but should; that's the deal about life. For young kids, though, experiences and opportunities come from only one source: adults must show them the doors.

Unfortunately, adults don't always bother.

A building contractor says: "We had about a half million perfectly smooth, perfectly clean, nice, even pieces of wood. Two by two, four, eight. Great building blocks for little people. We called three preschools in the neighborhood, told them to come pick them up. All said they would; none did."

A publisher: "Millions of junior high and high school kids seem interested in writing. 'How do I get my work published?', they ask. So we thought we'd give teenagers the opportunity to *get* published. We wrote to 22 schools around the country, asking teachers and counselors to invite students to contribute to a publication we were doing. We got an article from . . . *one!* student. Three of the schools flat-out declined, and the rest didn't even acknowledge us."

Before you holler about the schools not caring, you need to understand a point of public policy. Since you are The Public, that is pander-patter meaning you have helped slam the door on your kids.

It's this way. If I publish your student's essay, or print his picture in the paper, or use his name in a news release, I may be invading your privacy. If I single out your youngster for recognition — or if I do not — someone will believe I am exercising prejudice, favoritism, bending to special interest, or am guilty of some social/ political/ gender incorrectness or insensitivity. If I cast your offspring for any manner of performance public or private, and if he goofs up, you may believe I humiliated him. Our society has become so law-suited that more and more doors are no longer even approached, much less opened.

Since by policy we disallow the school to create experiences and make opportunities, then parents must assume most of the responsibility for doing so.

Most adults who work with kids do it with genuine, dedicated, sincere sense of influencing, imprinting, nurturing, of making a difference. Occasionally, some want *too much* to provide experiences; then it's the adults who have the experiences, not the kids.

When I went to summer camps as a pre-teen, we had to do "crafts." I *hated* crafts, and I weren't no good at it, neither. So my counselors always helped me. Those woven plastic-string necklaces and keychains were entirely the counselor's product, not mine, although the counselors always congratulated me when they finished. (Nobody said kids have to *like* everything they experience, or do well in all the things they explore. Part of the process is selecting out and turning down.)

At rest areas along the interstates, various organizations host the concession for Free Coffee (Donation Appreciated). One Saturday, Ourtown Rainbow Girls were on duty. All three RGs on duty remained submerged in paperbacks the whole time we were there, while their Daddy Advisor did all the work.

For years a farm couple had donated cash awards and trophies to local 4-H projects. "No more," they said. "We've discovered the parents do all the work. Awards in sheep raising have gone to kids who didn't have a clue about raising sheep."

You of course can plan and scrape and sacrifice and give your kids marvellous, rich experiences and wondrous opportunities. That's your responsibility, and that's the easy half of the equation.

The hard half is: The kids have to take them. Then they have to *do* something with them. That's *their* responsibility; and if they choose not to do it . . . it is . . . NOT . . . *your* fault! (Unless you pander them and do all the work for them.)

There are lots of knocks and some of them are nuisance calls, but it can't hurt to open the door and see. You never know whether it's the big, life-changing opportunity, or just the kitten scratching. Hey, listen: In 1963 the kids in a little Yukon River village hadn't seen a kitty before, so the one I brought them was, indeed, an opportunity to find out something new. So you see, what's old-mold for you can be the next great wonder of a child's world.

Finding the Doors

Every new thing a person sees, hears, and does, every new place he goes, every person he meets and every conversation he holds, every thing he finds out about is an opportunity to acquire information, fire an interest, spark imagination, form an attitude, spur creativity, discover an aptitude, develop a skill, instill a sense of the scheme of the physical and social world and the person's place in it, confirm or deny his sense of self-worth, and evaluate the meaning of it all.

Doorways to experiences and growth don't particularly come in different sizes, and most people fit in most doors. Libraries, zoos, ballgames, conversations, and making things are adaptable to all.

Specific suggestions are sprinkled throughout this book, but here are the general ideas.

❑ Talk with your kids. As in holding coherent conversations that have topics, not merely as in issuing orders. If you speak intelligently, they will respond with intelligence. By the time a youngster is 9 or 10, there's practically no such thing as talking over his head.

❑ Take your kids places. (But don't buy them stuff.)

❑ Get each child a library card. Nine months is a good age to start.

❑ Provide kids with things to do things *with.* Equipment for physical activity, art and craft supplies, and books for all ages. Toys for younger children; "real things" for older kids — tools, typewriter, trumpet, chessmen, and the like.

❑ Engage kids of all ages in everyday activites which develop attitudes, skills, and responsibilities. Food purchase and preparation, gardening, planning and scheduling of personal and family activities. Care and maintenance of home, car, yard, furnishings, equipment, personal and family space and possessions, and clothing. (Rough translation: chores!)

❑ Encourage school age kids to participate in classes and youth groups: day camps, programs at your local library and parks department; Scouting, Campfire, 4-H, Kids Inc., Job's Daughters, youth fellowship, little league (depending on the coach and the attitude on winning).

❑ Participate in community events and enrichment opportunities. Visit museums, galleries, exhibits, craft shows; attend the county fair, the Fourth of July parade and fireworks, the symphony and the church musicale, the annual Tour of Historical Homes; and sports events, science fairs, the band concert, and plays at the local school.

❑ Turn off the TV.

❑ Maintain your own interests, creativity, contacts, and skills. Demonstrate by your own example that these are worthwhile, lifelong endeavors; that there is breadth to life.

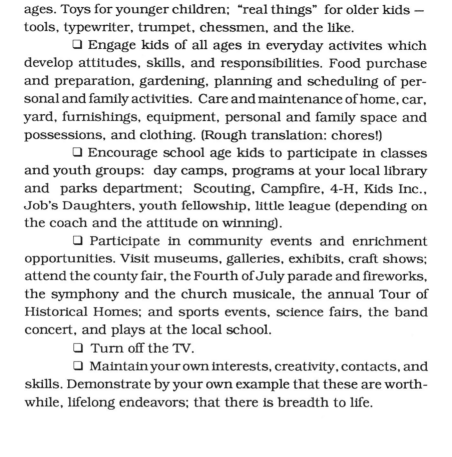

It's the adults' responsibility to show kids to the doors of experience and opportunity. It's the kids' responsibility to open them and go through.

3

Visitors day

The chains on the tires clanked a merry cadence as the big sedan we called the school bus carefully picked its way down the frozen slope of Mt. Hood, cutting through the icy shroud of February. Inside, on the warm back seat, I sat on my brother's warm, bundled-up lap, clutching a little brown teddy bear in one hand and a little brown sack of sandwiches in the other and I was thrilled chatterless. Last week I turned four, and now I could go to Visitors Day at Welches School.

We lived at Government Camp that winter, while my dad installed the wires and plugs that would bring power to a building-in-progress called Timberline Lodge. Every morning my dad put on his snowshoes and hiked up the mountain and every evening he strapped the snowshoes to his back and skied down the mountain to our rented cabin. My brother, a second grader, and Elaine and Skipper King, whose parents owned Battle Axe Inn, and another kid or two took the daily school bus ride and I was left behind. My best friend Skipper started school that year, leaving me deserted for the winter.

Welches School held regular Visitors Days and the kids always talked it up as a huge event, only you had to be a big four-year-old to go. Skipper went to Visitors Day last year and bragged about it all the time. Now I was big, too, and now I was about to enter That World.

"This is my sister," my brother told Miss Quigley. Ever since Elaine and my brother started first grade, Miss Quigley was the most famous name at Government Camp.

She grasped my hands and smiled and her eyes were shining lights. "I'm so happy you're here," she said, and I knew she meant it.

"I'm four now," I said. *She's pretty.* When my brother talked about her, he said, Miss Quigley She's Pretty, as if that were her full name.

We made a semicircle around Miss Quigley — right away I learned a new word, semicircle — and she read a story, holding the book so we could see the colorful pictures. *How can she read upside down and sideways?*

We sang. Little Sir Echo, how do you do? Hello ... (hello). Miss Quigley directed with her arms and hands, waving to this group — Hello — that group — (hello). Her wrists went *flop, flop* as she directed, and she taught us another new song. I'm going to leave ... *flop* ... (I'm going to leave ...) *flop* ... O-Old Texas now ... *flop* ... (Old Texas now ...).

"We're going to play a game. Make a circle." *Oh. Semicircle ... Circle.* "Join hands." *Oh. Hold hands. Join' means 'hold.'* "The farmer in the dell ... The farmer chews the wife." *Chews?* I understood The Dog Chews the Cat, but how come someone chews a wife? What's 'the dairyel'? *I don't know what some words mean. When I'm five I'll know all the words.*

Miss Quigley helped me bundle up, then wrapped my arms around my teddy bear. "I'm so glad you came."

I looked into her shining lights. "I'm going to be a teacher."

My teaching career began the next day. Every day, for the rest of the winter and spring of 1939, I arranged my toys in a circle and practiced my profession. "The doll chews the bear ..." and I directed Little Sir Echo and flopped my wrists just so. "Now boys and girls," I said in a smiling voice like Miss Quigley's, "let's write our numbers." Mrs. King let me hold the magazines in the enormous front room at Battle Axe Inn, and I practiced reading the pictures upside down and sideways.

In 1989, when Mrs. King was 83, I visited her at her home in Ocean Park, Washington. Coincidence: My best friend of early childhood was there. Skipper ... a Ph.D. and an outrageously handsome grandfather, a dead-ringer for his dad. *Time, I raise my arm to bid you slow down. I see only a hand, spotted and wrinkled.*

"A friend of mine saw Miss Quigley last month in Portland," Mrs. King said. "She's still pretty."

> An adult can never know at what moment she engraves a lasting imprint on a child. A word, a phrase, a look. An action, an attitude.

4

Sense of memory

. . . The answer, my friend, is blowin' in the wind.
The answer is blowin' in the wind.

What remembrances does that song call up? Do you
return to a place, a time . . . people? Who were you then? What
was the world then? In some way, Peter, Paul, and Mary were
part of who you were and what the world was, and when you
hear their songs today, the music carries you back to connect
your now with your then.

A peppery-haired man carrying a Notebook Computer
inside a briefcase of make-believe leather stands in a room and
when some people pass by he catches a whiff of something
subtly familiar. White Shoulders. *Her* fragrance. God, was it
that long ago? Memories tumble out like tennis balls spilling
from a locker, bouncing all around him. The scent carries him
to the campus, and he sees the trees and the dappled sunlight
on the vast expanse of lawn between buildings — they've
replaced the lawn with more buildings now. He hears the echoey
silence of the soaring-ceilinged library and he can smell books
and White Shoulders.

Sounds and scents evoke memories, but sometimes a
single word brings on the senses. Circus . . . *Circus.* Hear the
music? The roaring applause? See the blazing colors; the huge,
wrinkly elephants a-lumbering; the trapeeze lady with the frilly
costume shimmering in the spotlight; the clowns. Smell the
mustard and relish and cotton candy, and the animals. Feel the
warmth of lights and people and hot roasted peanuts in your
hand.

The other sense which makes us remember is the sense
of place. You read an item in the paper and you remember what
it said by visualizing its location on the page. When you hear the

item on the evening news, you again visualize the information as a place on a page. Your 9-year-old wails, "Where's my other shoe?" and you instantly recall having seen it beside the sofa. You hadn't actually noticed it when you saw it, but your mind registered an image of the shoe in a particular place.

Or: Who was it that told you how to prune your roses? Oh, yeah, it was Jim MacDonagal; I was sitting in that place at the table. I remember what he said because we were sitting right here, looking out the window . . .

Whenever I hear the word Phoenicians, I see a location. Not the Phoenicians' location. Mine, and Judy's, in the sixth grade. Judy sat two rows to my right, in the last desk. When Judy answered the teacher's question about the Phoenicians, I turned to watch Judy tell the teacher the Phoenicians had one of the earlier written languages, they were traders, merchants, and blenders of cultures, and they had remarkable boats. I remember the Phoenicians because I remember my spot and Judy's.

If these tricks work for us, you would think they ought to work for kids. They do.

Parents and teachers can make learning easier, and what is learned remain more firmly etched, by associating learning with the senses. On a stormy day, draw the kids' attention to the darkness and to the sounds of wind and rain at the same time you draw their attention to the business at hand. Some of them will remember that Helena is the capital of Montana because the rain spattered the windows. (And some of them will live out their lives thinking it's Joe, Montana, no matter what you tell them.)

Change the kids' places of business frequently. At home, different rooms, different chairs, studying under a different lamp. Reiterate the family rules while he ices a cake or while she sharpens the kitchen knives. At school, change the seating, vary the configuration of the room. If it sounds like too much work, consider it's a lot more efficient than going over and over the same old stuff.

For some of the really tough subjects, try it outside once in a while. *Seven times eight is fifty-six. I made a little pile of leaves on the ground.*

Capitalize on senses of sound and smell. Well, why *can't* they listen to Wagner while they fill in their outline maps of Europe? (If you can find a map of This Week's Version of Europe.) *Every time I hear "Ride of the Valkyries" my mind's eye sees Norway, Sweden, and Finland. I never forget the Scandinavians.* Boring things like subject-verb agreement might be much more palatable if served with the aroma of corn popping; and if the principal won't go for that, then you could wash down the dry subjects with some puckery juice, or maybe give each youngster a fresh, fragrant violet.

In fact, if principals or teachers have a problem with such interactive activities, then the students have a problem as well, because educators should understand and be able to apply the psychologies of learning. It may help to quote Dr. Marjorie Lachman, a psychologist at Brandeis University: "Sensory stimulation is essential to learning. The lack of stimulation may affect the chemical processes essential to good memory."

Okay — Again: What field are you in, what tree are you under, in what room do you sit, when you hear the answers blowin' in the wind?

> A sight, a song, a scent . . . let them carry you back. Remember who you were then, so you can know who your child is now.

5

The Main Ones

In this account of the social order of childhood, a writer from Idaho vividly recalls her status as a leftover.

Before lunch time my first day of first grade, I knew who The Main Ones were: Gail-and-Mary, Freddie-and-Bunny. You ran the names together, one word. In the third grade we moved to a new town, and there, again, before noon, I knew: Rae-and-Evelyn, Scott-and-Alan.

Always, The Main Ones held power, fearsome power which, by the age of 6 or 7, they had devised strategies to protect. It was they who decreed the correct dress, the right brand of crayons, the acceptable sandwiches and the approved lunch box; who designated how long you worked your arithmetic and the proper time to drop your completed paper on the teacher's desk. They determined who were In With The Main Ones and who were the leftovers. I was one of the leftovers.

Soon I figured it out: Main Ones had certain likenesses, as if there were requirements for belonging. All The Main Ones had 16 crayons in first grade, 48 by fourth; I started with eight and topped out at twenty-four. They all wore Captain Midnight Secret Decoder Rings, but my mom wasn't going to be taken in by any hero-endorsed promotions and she wouldn't buy Ovaltine; so I had no label to send in to get a Ring. Main Kids wore pretty clothes, different ones every day: a different dress, another shirt, clean and unfaded; Main Girls never needed safety pins to hold the broken elastic in their panties. The girls thought I was afraid to soar over the top on the Giant Strides, but the real reason I didn't Stride was because I needed one hand to hold my pants up. I'd rather they thought me scared.

None of The Main Girls had scabby knees from being clumsy, nor purple-striped legs from switchmarks, but I always had both. All girls wore dresses in the fifties, and everyone knew it when you fell down or got switched or when the elastic broke in your sox or underpants. None of the Main Girls had to wear knee-high sox in fourth grade, either. I think my mother made me wear those awful, old-fashioned long socks to hide the switchmarks. There was no such term as 'Child Abuse' then, and without definitions, things do not exist.

By fifth grade I had figured out something else. In a way I was glad to know, because it meant it wasn't my fault I was a leftover; but in another sense it was bad news, because it meant my status wouldn't change. I figured out that Main Kids belonged to Main Families, and they all had Main Mothers.

Main Mothers got permanents and wore lipstick to the store and they wore stockings you could see through, and delicate, unchunky high heels, and they belonged to Clubs, and they talked and laughed quietly. Main Families mowed their lawns, and their houses were clean and didn't stink. My mother said our house stunk because the man who lived there before us died in the bathroom; but a man died in the house across the street and that house didn't stink. Most of the Main Mothers were friends, and they talked about the creep mothers. I knew that because a couple of the kids told me what their Mothers said about mine.

The summer after seventh grade, I learned more memory verses than anyone else in Sunday School and I got the free trip to church camp for one week. From five counties the kids came, 75 of them, on equal terms, strangers all. No preconceptions. No Main Mothers, no leftovers. No baggage. How I looked forward!

Mrs. Craig, my Sunday School teacher, bought me a brand-new pair of jeans and two shirts to take to camp, and a for-real pair of tennis shoes, not the durable brown leather lace-ups of my mom's accustomed purchase, and I wore my new clothes and the kids found out I could sing and wisecrack and they liked me and after that I knew I would someday, somewhere, among someones, be some kind of a Main One on my own.

"They" will perceive your children the same way they perceive you. The advantage kids have is that they can overcome it.

6

All the other kids

"All the other kids have Hunker Rite Lite Boots.
I just HAVE to! PLEEEZE?"

"You aren't all the other kids."

I'm not ANY kid to you.

"Please, Mom, it's so important. ALL the kids have
Robbie Rapper CDs. Please, can't I get just one?"

"I don't care what ALL the kids do."

No, it isn't ALL the kids you don't care about. Just me.

"All the kids are wearing reversible neon jackets."

"So you don't want to eat meat, or what?"

No, I don't want meat. I'll eat beans, I'll do anything . . .

"All the kids have embossed sweatshirts. I really need
one, the one with the rubberized-plasticized flowers and the
kitten on the front."

"You don't NEED anything."

*You don't understand. I need it to fit in. To belong, I need
to belong.*

Drift your thoughts back, ten, fifteen years, twenty . . .
Old-looking faded blues were new then; or was it those trendy
expensive sport shoes, or the new state-of-the-art supersonic
boom box? The battles at home . . . *God, I'll never forget, you said
then.*

No, it wasn't ALL the kids — it was The Main Ones, the
trendsetters, the kids who . . . counted. You wanted to HAVE
those objects of battle — even if you didn't really want them. It
was what you needed to do — needed to do — to fit in the crowd:
you needed to belong.

As adults, we, too, strive to belong, to be like the other
kids. We conform. Sometimes it is so necessary to conform we
lose our jobs if we do not. When we're out with a group we order

what they order; you don't ask for prime rib and fries in the presence of sprout eaters. Our mode of dress, our language, our topics of talk are all determined by the group we are in. If you don't fit in you're an oddball.

And isn't that why, now, you tend the yard, sweep the porch, wash the car? Belonging, identifying, being identified. Isn't that why you give a gift you can scarcely afford to a bride you scarcely know; why you send Christmas cards to the right people; why you go to the right mall to be seen?

If an adult fails to fit in he is called weird. If weird is traumatic to a forty-year-old, imagine how it must smart to a youngster who hasn't the experience to cope.

How do we so soon forget?

I began teaching at a new high school the same year my lastborn entered it as a freshman. We started school together. We both had a new set of norms to figure out. By noon of the first day, I had at least one thing figured.

"All the kids are using Trapper Keepers," I told her at home that evening. "You need one."

Her eyes widened, her brows shot upward. "I don't *need* one; they're twelve-ninety-five. Are we quitting meat, or what?"

"You need a Trapper Keeper. We'll eat beans."

Some things should be forever remembered.

What kids "need" . . . is to belong.

7

The alibi institute

My first term in college I took Psych 101 and the first thing they told us in psych was: If a kid messes up it's the parents' fault.

I felt cheated. I had missed out on going-on 19 years of Scapegoat Opportunity. All those years, at real regular intervals, my dad had peered at me from inside his bushy eyebrows and intoned in that deep, Masonic-Lodge-Ritual voice, "That's no excuse, Susan!" And, dummie me! I believed him. And here I find out I could have been getting away with murder and not had to take the rap myself.

In Sociology Four-forty-something, the prof decreed that crooks and deviants were: Society's Fault. So, well, if not murder, I should have been at least getting away with shoplifting — times were tight for us then, two kids and one income and me still an undergrad and all.

I had already found out, in Education 200: If a kid messed up, it was the teacher's fault.

I wished I had known *that*, the day we did sulfur dioxide in chemistry (you know, the rotten eggs thing). I hadn't quite precisely followed exact instructions and half the guys on the second floor wound up losing their Wheaties and Mr. Boyd and everyone else blamed *me*; and I, not realizing there were textbooks out there saying it was *his* fault, accepted all the blame. So without even filing a grievance, I took my flunk in sulphur dioxide.

When my Number One Kid got in trouble in junior high, he scowled from behind his brows the way my dad did and said defiantly: "It's your fault." When asked what makes him think that, he raised his brows and lowered his lids to half-mast and said haughtily: "When people mess up, it's the mother's fault. I read it in *Newsweek*."

This was about the time the Beat Generation was busy absolving itself with I Don't Know Who I Am, and I Didn't Ask To Be Born. We heard those also from Number One, who read them in *U.S. News & World Report.*

So now the Scapegoat Information was out of the towers of higher education and into the public press. So now anyone who could read could go do anything he wanted and get away with it.

A kid doesn't even have to read to catch the alibis. Some years ago a mom and dad and their four-year-old visited us one eveninng. Everyone thought the child was around genius level because the mom said he was.

Abruptly and without any apparent precipitation, the kid cut loose a scream, began crying and stamping his feet about 180 beats per minute, then turned round and round in tight little circles, still hollering. With equal abruptness he quit and returned to the sofa, and you got the distinct impression his little hissie was deliberately staged. Calmly the young genius announced, "I'm just . . . stressed . . . *out.*"

(Shortly after this the mom and dad split. There was said to have been quite a battle over genius-custody. It was also said the loser got him.)

If you can't find anyone to blame, you can at least make it okay. Confess, repent, be forgiven. Once, one of my little ruffian third graders explained sweetly, "I can do anything I want. All I have to do is tell the priest and it's okay." This spring we had a long visit with one of Ruffian's classmates (who's older now than I was then), who told us Ruffy is currently in jail.

Today there is a rich, creative array of excuses for every circumstance, and a huge bevy of counselors, organizations, clinics, centers, support groups, agencies, journalists, journals, authors, and booksellers to define and treat them. It's booming big biz.

We have seen the institutionalization of excuses.

Today's leading reasons for messing up: stress; lack of self-esteem; sexual harrassment (even though it happened 27 years ago, before they invented the term, and you don't quite recall the exact person, place, or words; excuses are retroactive). Dysfunctional families: my uncle/ grandfather/ cousin's wife is alcoholic. Sexual abuse in childhood (more meaningful if you're a celebrity). The job is wrong for me our schools are no good our society is in hell.

Society sanctions and provides instruction in a raft of other alibis, too. Punishment; no punishment; poverty; affluence; mom works; mom doesn't work; credit cards; computer error; government; government forms; national leadership; local leadership; the Japanese; God's will.

Some of these are real reasons. We are not making light of real lives in real trouble. The thing is, everyone tries to catch the wave. The young person who's rebellious and irresponsible because he didn't ask to be born is not in the same league with the beaten-up child. But . . . give Rebel a hi-sound psycholabel like Negative Acceptance Syndrome and you've given "Didn't Ask To Be Born" some useful dysfunction value.

We have so institutionalized our excuses that there's a psych-tech one for every occasion, and a counseling-and-support group to validate it. What was once a gossamer cop-outing is now a viable member of the system.

The evening before the day the errants' names were announced in the 1992 U.S. House Banking Scandal (a.k.a. Rubbergate), a U.S. Rep who had boomeranged a few thousand in tissue-paper checks appeared on MacNeil-Lehrer. He blamed the whole thing on the House bank, which let the Honorable Representatives get away with rubber writing. Not the Congressmen's fault; it's the bank's. A Republican who spent some bouncies said it was the Democarts' fault, since the Democrats are the House majority.

A couple of our acquaintence was raising a foster daughter. By 15, the girl grew waywarder and waywarder and was at last placed in a group home having full-time, intensive-care counselors.

"I went to visit her the other day," my friend told me. "And do you know what she said? She said, 'Mom, I have issues. They told me I have *issues*.' Can you believe that? The shrinks at the juvenile home aren't telling kids they'd better straighten up and fly; they're telling them they have ISSUES."

For a couple of weeks I eavesdropped on a computer bulletin board for teenage poets, writers and artists. There was considerable agreement among them: "I'm kind of weird because I'm so creative."

Well, yeah, you'll have to admit that's creative, all right. But bless you, my children: At least you aren't out there blaming everyone and everything and God. And catch the new day dawning, sisters — they aren't even blaming their mothers.

> Excuses have become institutionalized into big biz. Every haywire from laze to lust is hi-psych bogglebabble now. . .and you're no-fault, if you buy a counselor and join a support group.

8

Your gender and socially correct child

The month before Pearl Harbor, I took home my first report card. It was a light green 8.5-by-11-inch sheet folded to make three pages of print and a cover, and the three pages were filled with my teacher's assessments of various Minnie Mouse attributes. My first grade report card didn't report how well I could read and spell, which I could do; but whether I could draw nicely and peel my morning fruit without making a mess and sit still and be quiet for an hour and a half, which I could not. (In case you thought skipping the academics has been stylish only since the seventies.)

All those attributes were written up in little incomplete sentences, which even a six-year-old could figure was a bit cute from an institution aiming for literacy. "Keeps his things in his own space". . . "Cleans up after himself". . . "Waits his turn. . ." (Sounds like Robert Fulghum's *All I Really Need to Know I Learned in Kindergarten* list, say what? See — the basics haven't either changed.)

"And why," I asked my mother, "did I get someone else's report card? I'm not a him."

Well, things have changed, sort of. It is no longer Gender And Socially Correct to refer to people with the once genderless, grammatically correct pronouns *he, him, his, himself*. How far has the "correctness" boomerang boomered? Last week I read two different raising-your-kid type magazines cover to cover — ads, articles, letters to the editor, and all. The generic child was referenced by the generic pronoun *he* only three times. All other pronouns were the genderless, generic feminine versions. So N.O.W. it's the boys who think they got the wrong report card.

One thing the Gender Correcters don't seem to get is that girls are willing to identify with the male persona but boys won't accept the feminine versions. Girls love Sherlock Holmes and Tom Sawyer, but a boy wouldn't be caught with a Nancy Drew, and forget Anne of Green Gables. The only way they get all the kids to "read" Dick and Jane is to make Dick the older one, the leader. First Dick says "Oh, look and see," then Jane parrots. I know a raft of girl writers who use masculine pen names, but, except for a few men who crack the romance-and-confessions market for a lark, men don't take on names like Melissa and Bambi. Moms proudly brag if their daughters are tomboys, but just let anyone call their man-child a sissy.

The other thing the All Persons Are Created Equal movers have overlooked is: the sexes are *not* created equal. Boy newborns and girl newborns wet their diapers in different spots, and after that, girl toddlers are housebroken earlier and easier. Girls walk younger and talk sooner, and boys are physically stronger and they do better with building blocks and puzzles.

Almost always, you can distinguish male and female penmanship. In fact, a look at handwriting gives us a strong clue as to which sex seems to have the stronger flocking instinct: all the girls in junior high and high school write alike. If you want to identify the real individualists, find the penmanship which dares to be distinctive.

From infancy through the teens, girls are more likely to excel in language skills, boys at mathematics and geometry (except that left-handed girls are likely to understand math on a par with their male agemates). In fact, boys' whole perception of mathematics, space, and shape is different. When they build with blocks, boys create towering structures and girls construct enclosures, says Pam Brono, coordinator of the Child Development Center at Mt. Hood Community College, Gresham, Oregon.

Ms. Brono instructs workshops for persons who work with preschoolers. At one, a participant was a pre-school teacher with a class of eight 3-year-old boys and one girl; another taught a four-year-old group of 19 boys and one girl. Now, an individual enlightened in late-twentieth-century theory of equality of the sexes might respond, "So what's the problem?" The pre-school professionals in Ms. Brono's workshop responded, "Plenty of problems. Nineteen of them."

Males and females are wired differently. Wired, literally: the electrical circuitry in the brain — *brains:* left and right — are connected differently in hims and hers. From the second fetal trimester onward, females' electrical impulses cross the chasm between hemispheres more effectively. As a result, girls gain language skills and fine muscle coordination earlier than little boys; women recover from strokes faster and more completely than men.

Stated in what are probably the least diplomatic terms: women use more of their brains than men.

Masculine logic, feminine intuition? It's true. They're plugged in that way. Star Trek got it right in casting Spock as a man and Counselor Troi, a woman.

Furthermore, southpaws are wired differently than right handers, and the learning process is different for each. In addition, righties who have a left-handed parent or sibling learn by different routes than righties whose relatives are all right-handed. That is the conclusion of Thomas Bever, professor of psychology and linguistics at the University of Rochester, who has researched handedness and learning patterns.

"He's *All Boy!* " brags the parent. Well, we hate to break your bubble, but boys are not all male.

See, there are these chromosomes, X and Y. They always march two-by-two, and they determine human sex.

If XX march together, it's a girl.

If X and Y get together, it's a boy.

There is no such thing as YY, because women do not have a Y chromosome. Since all babies have mothers, everyone gets an X, because that's the only kind mothers have to give. If the dad contributes one of his X's to the mother's X, the child is a girl. If the dad sends in a Y, it's a boy.

A girl is X X. A boy is XY. He is half X; he can not be All Boy.

But don't get all bent out, guys. There's no All Girl, either. Females produce testosterone. That's why your grandma has whiskers.

They even have ways of legislating your correct ethnicity. When a friend of mine, one of the horde of fleeing Californians, migrated outward, there was a recession on. As a last resort, when he was job-hunting, he decided he may as well claim his opportunity for Equal Opportunity Employment. "I'm half Hispanic," he told the bureau of employment opportunity in his new state.

"Do you speak Spanish?"

"No."

"Then you're not Hispanic."

"But I speak Deutsche."

"That is not an advantage. Germans are not disadvantaged." The state opportunist check-marked the square: Bilingual — No.

"In the Willamette Valley, 'bilingual' means English and Spanish," my friend found out later. "Unless you're Native American, in which case you can be bilingual if you speak Chinook Jargon, although there's no bureaucratic call for Chinook bilingualism."

Things do change. There was a time when being German was a flaw. At the beginning of World War One my dad's family changed its nationality to Dutch.

Today's socially-correct journalists now have to refer to the smallest of people by last name only. They hide gender-revealing first names like Joshua or David or Mary Anne. "Baby Smithe was born Tuesday. Smithe weighed 7 pounds. Smithe was named Hannah Joanna."

Then there's the social correctness that says no child is too young to be endowed with adult status. "A 12-year old man and a 10-year-old woman won the spelling bee."

So if the newspaper confers them with adulthood, well, hey, why *shouldn't* they take over the household?

People aren't created quite the same, but we have to make them identically socially neutral and identity-nothing.

9

Stars twinkling, and space

At two and a half, Joyce had not spoken her first words. She's a late bloomer, her mother said; see how she interacts, you can tell she comprehends. No, she's speech impaired, her grand aunt said; see how she reaches but cannot make the words come out.

Two months before her third birthday, Joyce said her first words. Her first was "eat. " Her second word was "shopping" — honest, I am not making that up. Her third word was Twinkle-twinkle-little-star-how-I-wonder . . . The entire thing as one word, recited completely, accurately, and intelligibly. Her next word was Row-row-row-your-boat-gently-down-the-stream-merrily. . . After that she chanted, sang, and said rhymes and stories. From memory. Completely, accurately, and intelligibly.

In a village in one of America's pockets of poverty lived little Charlotte, four years old and speechless. She wandered the town, random-motioned and apparently without connection to anything, anywhere. She's probably aphasic, the town teachers armchair-diagnosed; she lacks either the brain circuits or the physical apparatus to process language, or even to concentrate.

Over the summer, when the teachers were gone and thus missed the miracle, Charlotte began talking. In sentences, paragraphs, in daylong chatter. The words came, and when they did, they expressed ideas, bodies of knowledge, and awareness of people and what people are like. Her ideas were immature and her knowledge rudimentary, but no less so than other children her age in that particular setting. Head Start proved a catalyst for Charlotte's metamorphosis, and the kindergarten and first grade teachers blessed Head Start for its wonders, because by first grade Charlotte had caught up to her agemates.

Gofer (I forget his real name; but then, he's probably forgotten me, too) sort of spent classes in 10-Forward, trekking off in some galactic sphere. He didn't acknowledge transmissions to his communicator; and his assignments . . . you know.

But his classroom tests! Not just simple, ordinary flying colors; they were prisms of light. And standardized achievement tests? Did I mention the stratosphere? He never appeared to expend an ounce of energy matter studying, and on paper he put only the minimum requirements to sustain life; but even off exploring unknown worlds, he osmosised just about everything of this earth.

This was Christine's third year in the nursing home. When I happened to be in town, I went to visit. She was my seventh grade music teacher, the one who taught me to play the trombone, and who imprinted me with so many of the intangibles that sustain kids through the awful years of adolescence. (Why do they call high school "the wonderful time of your life"?) Christine never got around on a trombone herself, but she clarinetted in the Women's Army Corps symphonic band, and she did awesome piano and organ. Through the years I had kept up the friendship, though this was the longest time I had gone without seeing her.

When I arrived at the home, Dave was there, as he was every day. "She won't know you," he told me as he led me to her room. "She doesn't know anything any more. She's been out in space for two years now."

When we stepped into Christine's room, she looked at me hollow-eyed, without a flicker of recognition, as Dave had warned she would. Then she smiled. "I was out there playing my trombone," she said, tilting her head toward the gathering room. "The old people said I was too loud, so I had to come back in here. Who are you?"

The past twenty-five years have brought enormous gains in our understanding of the human mind and of thought and learning, but so much is not yet known. How does information get there? How is it stored? How is it retrieved? Why is it not able to get out? What finally triggers the firing pins so that all the systems connect?

Maybe it's time to rethink some ideas. We believe that learning must be interactive; that for kids to *learn,* they must *work* at it, and *concentrate* and *pay attention* and *answer my questions.* So if all that attentive concentration is required, how come those subliminal messages on TV are illegal?

How do we account for the phenomenal success of Sesame Street, where the learning that takes place is not interactive at all, but in fact it comes pretty close to subliminality. Yet for almost twenty years now, kindergarten and first grade teachers all over America have said they could identify in an instant the kids who grew up on Sesame Street — the ones who know the most and are best equipped to progress the fastest.

And how can we explain that a 6-year-old is declared "Not ready to read. Does not distinguish symbols such as d-b, q-g-p, 1-1" — while that same child, since he was a year and a half, could identify the Golden Arches, differentiate the symbols for K-Mart and Circle K; Pizza Hut and Pietro's; tell by looking whether it was bran flakes or Wheaties; and know which were the dime store shoes and which were Nikes?

Children like Joyce and Charlotte show us that little stars do twinkle and expand in the mind, even though their lights cannot shine outwardly.

People like Gofer demonstrate that galaxies of information seep in without effort or awareness, like radiation from outer space enters, undetected.

Thousands of Christines suggest that something of what was once there may still be. Floating in space, perhaps; but sometimes contact is made. We may never realize what contact, nor with whom.

> We do not not fully understand how humans learn, but learning is happening and is being remembered when we think it is not. Perhaps it would be a good idea to approach every person — the very young, the very old, the apparently disabled— as though they were taking it all in.

2

Because I'm the Grown-up
Here, That's Why

A place to grow

10

The family track and heroes

"When my grandmother died, my grandfather didn't have the first idea what to do with children," says a woman in Minnesota. "So the five kids, aged 4 through 15, were farmed out to anyone who would take them." That happened in 1925.

"When I was ten, my mother was bedridden for three months," recalls a man from British Columbia. "My 7-year-old sister and I washed dishes and swept and dusted, and a high school girl came in to do the cooking and laundry while my dad read the paper and puttered in his shop. He didn't participate in caring for the new baby; mom did it from her bed. Men did not do house chores and they didn't take care of babies." That was 1942.

"When I was in high school, my mom visited my brother in Maryland for two weeks," says a Washington woman. "I did the housework and cooking. My semi-retired dad had a part-time business at home, but certain things were 'women's work' and he did not do them." That was 1951.

A North Carolina executive says, "When my girls were school age, my job required my taking four or five trips a year. Before each trip I filled the freezer with casseroles and desserts, and sometimes the children stayed overnight with friends. My husband was a terrific cook, and he was fond of the girls; but he considered kids and cooking as recreational things, not steady obligations." This was between 1966 and 1975.

For over a generation now, "everyone" has decried the deterioration, disintegration, breakup, breakdown, and dissolution of America's families, and the increased absence of fathers in households. Is it too radical to suggest that "everyone" makes too much ado about too little? If you are over 40, the chances are the father in the household didn't participate much in the the management of family and home, anyway.

The facts: Male role models are stronger and more plentiful today than in 1960. The dads who are present today are more actively involved in the imprinting, bonding, and nurturing of children. Now, says Pamela Stebbeds Knowles, partner in the West Coast law firm Davis Wright Tremaine, "It isn't a Mommy Track any more. It's a Family Track. More men are stopping and telling the corporate world they are sharing in family life and parenting."

In 1955, the Selah, Washington schools hired a male fourth grade teacher, the first man in that district to request a grade lower than fifth. By the end of that decade men were teaching lower grades throughout the Yakima Valley. It pleased administrators and delighted moms to have "male role models for the children, since so many kids' dads are so uninvolved." In that era dads were there, but they were hardly there.

By National Education Association figures, 1,218,659 women and 212,992 men taught grades K through 6 in America's public schools in 1991-92. (Surprisingly, NEA doesn't break out the numbers by grade level.) The elementary grades, especially K through 3, were once a women's bastion, but men have entered it because they realize it's important for young children to have a male constant in their lives . . . and guys have also discovered they like little kids.

Children of disintact familes of the 90s may actually receive more active fathering than kids in unbroken ones of the 50s and 60s. Shared custody "is becoming fairly widespread," report various children's service agencies, although none can come up with any specific figures. When shared custody is awarded, it is because fathers petition for it. No; they fight for it. And those dads are more active, more involved, more consciously nurturing parents than the domestically passive men of the Golden Years of The Family.

Similarly, the number of kids living with the father-only has increased. In 1960, the count was 724,000, or 1.1 percent of American children. In 1989, the latest statistical year, it was 1,793,000, for 2.8 percent. The courts no longer automatically and unquestioningly award custody to the mother.

Kids don't call them "role models," they call them Heroes. Kids' heroes are mostly men. Since 1980 *The World*

Almanac has taken an annual Hero Poll of America's teenagers. From the kids' Hero List we can surmise that teen-agers have swung around from the world of entertainment to the world that's real. From 1980 through 1988, their Heroes were all male, all actors. In 1989 they shifted from stage to court, when they named Michael Jordan their top choice, and in 1990 it was singer-dancer-choreographer Paula Abdul, the first woman to become the teens' Number One Hero. That year, the second place winner was another lady, the one kids call "Mom." Jordan was number three, and fourth, "Dad." Dad is still a presence, whether he's present or not.

In 1991, American teens looked up to people of substance. Julia Roberts, in second place, was the only screen personality in the top five. The Number One Man: General H. Norman Schwarzkopf. Third, George Bush; fourth, Jordan again; and fifth, Barbara Bush, the teens' most popular First Lady ever.

Results of another poll were announced in January, 1992, and this one included responses of elementary students as well as high schoolers. The students' Most Admired Person: President Bush. George Bush is a positive influence on the emotional health of Americans, says Peggy Noonan in her book *What I Saw at the Revolution* (Ivy Books, 1990). "Words that have special meaning for him: Family, kids, grandkids, love, decency . . . kindness, caring . . . excellence." Bush, and Reagan before him, says Noonan, demonstrated that it's all right to show you care, and it's all right to cry.

Teens' selection of Mom, Dad, the Bushes, Schwarzkopf, and Sandra Day O'Connor (in 1991, Ms. O'Connor and Ms. Abdul tied for tenth place) suggest that not only do Nineties Kids admire people of substance, but that age and experience have value also.

American dads? There's plenty of evidence that, even considering all the fathers who are not physically present in the home, more men actively participate in parenting now than when "American families stayed together." And if you total up the quality of male parenting, role models, and heroes . . . no contest at all.

11

The broken family mold

At a family get-together, five women visited. Three mothers in their late twenties and two grandmas, the younger womyne's moms.

The talk quickly turned to parenting, as it does when mothers meet (and not so much when fathers do). When should you . . . What do you do about . . . Why does . . .?

"We don't know the right answers," said the grandmothers. Parenting is a hard job.

One of the young mothers directs an agency which, in cooperation with a local community college, arranges child care for teen-age mothers attending high school classes, and educates them in parenting.

It's so difficult being a teen parent, the younger women murmur. A girl has to cancel her life and there's no father around to help. And teenagers don't know how to raise a child.

"Weren't you listening?" asked one of the grandmothers. "Nobody knows, not even us old people. You don't automatically have all the answers just because you get some seasoning in life."

"The problem," said the director, "is that the girls may not want help. They feel they're being singled out. Okay, discriminated against. The five of us, right here right now, just demonstrated that we all have the same questions, and it's not just teen-agers who don't have the answers. Being a mother is not different for them."

History and demographics strongly suggest she is correct.

Since the dawn of humankind, teenagers bore children. At fifteen, sixteen . . . twenty was late for a first child. This was so until quite recently, within the past hundred years. In the big gestault of human society, ours is not the overall average. Girls learned mothering from their mothers, their grandmothers. Was parenting easier then? Did they do a better job? Did our foremothers have better answers than we have?

Or were the questions different?

Today's teens have no corner on single parenthood. According to one Bureau of the Census figure, 15,867 American children, or 24.7 percent of all children under age 18, lived with one parent in 1990. The other figure says that 30.6 percent lived with a parent who had never been married. (The fact that one agency gives two different figures in the same report indicates the fallibility of statistics!)

Nor do teens constitute the greatest percentage of unmarried mothers. In 1988, the latest year's figures from National Center for Health Statistics, 9,907 babies were born to unmarried girls under 15 years; 312,499 to girls aged 15 to 19 (3.6 percent of unmarried females in that age group). But 682,893 single women over age 19 gave birth; and of these, 129,282 (1.72 percent of age group) were in their thirties.

The largest percentage of unmarried mothers were ages 20 to 24 (5.67 percent of unmarried females in that age group); and ages 25 to 29 (4.81 percent). According to the Federal Centers for Disease Control, "The sharpest increases in birthrates from 1980 to 1988 were among older women. The birthrate among single women age 15 to 17 years rose 29 percent; the rate for ages 30 to 34 rose 52 percent."

As far as the presence of a father, there are no figures to reflect the men who are inactive in the child-rearing process. Historically, dads haven't participated much in parenting, anyway. Until the 1950s, fathers did not parent; they provided. Before that, throughout personkind's wars, which have gone on quite steadily for millenia, mothers raised children alone. Yet it has been only since the 1950s that families have been called broken if two parents do not actively participate.

Granted, any teen or any other single mother must put her life on hold for children. But so do all of us, unless we're very rich or very royal.

The irony of our humanness is that raising a child is the hardest thing to do, and having a baby is the easiest. Being a parent is the only major career requiring no qualifications and no prior training.

Things have changed. Perhaps the questions are the same, but all their contexts are different now. So we get caught up trying to define as problems things that haven't always been problems, in establishing an "average" when there is none. We say This is how it should be, and if it's not that way it's broken. The director of the children's agency, who constantly reassesses and re-questions her own parenting, says, "I might be sitting in the cynic's seat — but the business of defining social issues *is* a business. A major growth industry. You declare a problem, you add to the payroll."

Then she says, "I think what we do best is to make girls feel embarrassed and inadequate. I think we — the social we — are trying to squeeze society into a mold that should be thrown away."

> *They* tell us what our families should be like. But very few of us are A Family As It Should Be. It's time to recompute the "average," to recast the mold.

12

Returning to the family, in business

In droves and herds, Mothers of the Nineties are leaving the workplace to stay home with their flocks. Nineties Dads take paternity leave when their babies are born and sick leave when they are ill, and turn down promotions that would mean longer hours and farther distances from home. I haven't been able to find any statistics that actually verify the trend as a fact. But when both Gannett and *Time* talk trend, then it's a trend.

Columnists, call it a "movement" — everything is; and it has a name — everything does. "The Return to the Family."

Its implication is erroneous. Can we return to where we never left?

Some women are quitting work to become "full-time mothers." (Gobbledygook. Motherhood is permanent, not just when you and the kids are home together. That sort of jargontalk is like saying you're part-time Norwegian, or you're fat only when you look in the mirror.)

In actual fact, most "returning" mothers are having the second or third child, and the cost of child care equals their take-home. Sometimes more. Women who "have" to work are the ones most likely to have jobs that don't pay enough for food, home, insurance, and child care. There could be a movement back to the family, yes. But a good share of that comes from minimum pay more than from a dying desire to be a full-timer.

The head of a lower-middle level agency (okay, a bureaucrat) was elated when she received a raise to seven-ten an hour. That isn't bad pay this year in this state — check out the classifieds and see. Still, after taxes that's the lower end of five dollars, minus another buck and a half for child care. When the second baby arrives, that will be another $2, because infants cost more than preschoolers. Plus car, clothes, and collections at the office. Yes, she's "returning home." Working motherhood is a Crunch-22.

Along with this is another "movement," according to the newsmags, the womyne mags, and the business advisories. Work At Home. Start Your Own Home Business. Ponder it a minute and you see it's ludicrous, impractical, illogical, and unworkable. But it obviously sells magazines. And it sells This Colorful, Informative Pamphlet For Only $15.95 Plus A $2 Handling Fee.

First of all, starting a business takes capital, even though some endeavors may require only a "small amount." Even the most modest start-up seldom comes under $2000. Anyone who "has" to work lacks the capital to start up company dinner, much less a home secretariat.

Second, the theory in the magazines goes that Moms can devote full time to child rearing and then squish in their home-working hours at their convenience. One of the oversights here is . . . did you ever try to actually accomplish intellectual concentration around a toddler? The other is . . . did you ever hear of a successful business which was launched on a part-time basis?

I would like to suggest that the full-time Returnee-to-the-Family who combines a Business At Home will spend less time with the children than she did when she worked eight hours a day and commuted. I read computer network exchanges among a score of women who had established some sort of home business — usually secretarial, editorial, or "party" sales plans. Guess what was their biggest problem. The need for help. Guess how they solved it. Hiring a sitter to come to the house.

One mother wrote that she had a high school girl come in to hold the baby so she, the mother, had a chance to get the chores done. Now, let's see . . . why was it the woman quit working?

There is a prevailing notion that what kids really need and what they really want is to have Mom at home. The notion has prevailed since the forties that I know of, so no doubt it was around before that.

In nineteen sixty-something I visited the home of one of my seventh grade students. I went there because his mother didn't come to see me on conference day, and my principal "suggested" that since it was on my way . . . I arrived about five in the afternoon. Mom was watching the game shows. The stacks of stuff around the sofa included, among other things, full ashtrays, empty bottles, candy wrappers, and love-and-adultery magazines. But I sound snippy. Of course a boy needs a full-time mother who's there when he gets home.

"They" (meaning the columnists, I think) say that kids would rather have mom at home to talk to than have "things" mom's working-money can buy. Baloney! Kids would rather have boom boxes, brand-name jeans, and time and space. And what kids over age 11 (A) are home during waking hours; or (B) talk to adults when they *are* home?

We are told that kids get messed up because their mothers work; but all of us have known plenty of messed up kids whose mothers have never received a pay slip.

We are told that kids get messed up because of poverty, that they need more advantages, more opportunities, more cash to work their way up with, and that their mothers should stop staying home and go get a job. But we all know very strapped people who did *not* mess up.

There are too few correlations. For every illustration of Up there's an equal one for Down. The one conclusion "they" seem to miss is that kids are the way they are because they're kids.

It's sort of like saying The sun rises if you sleep on your left side . . . No, the sun rises if you sleep on your right side. Wrong twice. The sun rises, period. Some kids turn out. Period.

All this may seem to be lightly taken, but it isn't. So much of what we think is up, down, in, out, and trendy is decreed by so few of "them." A lot of us do what we do, in spite of the trends, because we have to. Or, by God, because we want to.

Never mind the trends. It's possible that the trends don't exist; and it's probable that they are based on flawed assumptions. Parenting is not simply a matter of putting in your time, and some of the highest-quality time is that full-attention half-hour.

Journalist George Will disagrees with me on this, however: "It isn't *qualitative* time kids want," he writes. "It's *quantitative.* They want their parents to give them more time of any kind."

However, this has been validated: parents who work are four times more likely to spend that quality time with children.

Do your own thing for your own reasons. But tell yourself what your real reasons are.

Start a business you can spend more time with the baby? Don't get covered with snow.

Whether you work because you have to, or because you want to, go do it; and don't ever again feel guilty about doing it.

13

The crunch generation

Once upon a time, long ago in the United States, young people graduated from high school, worked their way through college, immediately gained lucrative employment in the field where their hearts were, and more or less prospered. A house, multiple cars, professional credentials, perhaps in time a business of their own which, compared to today, was relatively free of regulations and prohibitions.

If you are young enough to have preschoolers or primary graders, you probably believe that such a time is known only to history majors.

If you are thirty-five or under, the chances are you have lived with your folks at some time since high school. Some seventy percent of you have, whether you graduated from college or not. Not by choice; by paradox: you were the ones who couldn't wait to get . . . out . . . of this HOUSE!

I have met hundreds of people of your parents' generation, and almost all of them, at some time or another and for varying durations of time, housed one, two, or all their adult kids. (Where are the thirty percent who were *not* forced to move back home?) I'll tell you this: Very few of the old folks really, terribly minded. One reason they didn't mind is that, after you said all those things about squares over thirty who didn't know anything, they felt warm and furry that you would return to the house you couldn't wait to get out of. The other reason is that they see how times have changed, how tough it's been for you to get yourselves set up, and they feel some twangs of injustice that things were so damn easy for *them.*

Easy, indeed. People who reached adulthood in the bustling, busting late forties and the fifties were of a generation of sparse births. There were simply more jobs then than workers. *What do you want to do? Okay, what city do you want to do it in?*

It was a whale of a lot easier socially, too. There have always been peer pressures, but people who are fifty didn't come close to having it like people who are thirty. If you're somewhere between legal age and forty, dwell on this one awhile: Your parents are the last drug-free generation in America.

And, Thirtysomethingers, what about your kids? As if it weren't enough to contend with the spectre of drugs, gangs, an atrocity of a health care situation, a pratt-flat economy, and an educational system that might best be fixed with a bulldozer and a match, there's the matter of college.

As we head into the mid-nineties, a couple of sets of numbers are out. One says that if your youngster is a preschooler now, the price for her four-year education at an "average" private university in the United States will be $240,000. The other, quoted in widely distributed public service announcements designed to encourage kids to stay in school, says, "College graduates earn a quarter of a million dollars more in their lifetime than drop-outs." Spend a quarter, earn a quarter. Pretty close to break-even, isn't it?

The current popterm for the parents of twentyish to thirty-somethingers is The Sandwich Generation. Here's a name for yours: The Crunch Generation. You're probably still paying off your student loans from college; and, if you're a statistical average, you don't yet own a home and you're grasping and grappling in a deteriorating job market. Now, any dummy can see that a family who plans to have a quarter of a mill scraped up for college is going to have to start scraping. Starting about five years ago. Given all your other circumstances, a fair question is: What's to scrape up?

Given all this, it seems a certainty that by the year 2020 the collective *We* will have changed our views about higher education. In the first place, if a person has $240,000 lying around, he doesn't *need* college. Or, families who don't have it will decide it's cheaper to just keep supporting the kid; and in that case, she doesn't need college, either.

But wait. Don't jump off the bridge yet. There are now and will surely continue to be ways around the awful prohibitiveness of higher education.

— The 240 figure is for *private* schools. The ticket for state schools is projected to remain comparatively lower — only about $150,000 by 2020. By another source's numbers, public schools will cost only about $27,000 per year by then.

— Community colleges have not only established themselves as places of meat-and-guts academia, they do it for less. The pros predict your nearby two-year-school will continue to be the source of your best postsecondary educational bargain, though the bargain will continue to be relative to the costs of other types of schools.

— Grants, scholarships, work-study programs, and student loans will be continued; people who go around predicting things say these programs will "keep relatively abreast of increasing costs."

However, as costs escalate, the necessity for such assistance will increase also, and competition for aid will toughen. The lesson to hammer in is: Achieve. More and more, I suspect, the freebies will go to the proven producers.

Concerning the price of a degree now, in the 1990s, Charles Mullins, a counselor at Sullivan Central High School, Blountville, Tennessee, says firmly: "There are so many programs available that no qualified person should have to forego college due to lack of funds." Mullins adds, "Don't fall for software for computerized 'fund searches.' They are ripoffs."

— Several states issue college bonds called baccalaureate bonds. Purchased from individual states for too-good-to-be-true prices and maturing in 10 to 18 years, depending on your specific plan and payment, bac bonds guarantee full-fare payment for four years attendance at a postsecondary school in the state.

Bac bonds come with limits, of course. In most states, they can be purchased only by the child's parents, although grandparents could certainly give gifts of money with which to buy the bonds. The bonds are redeemable only as direct payment to the college the child attends. They honor only state-operated institutions in the state issuing the bond.

If you choose to buy bac bonds for your children, then naturally you will not bring them up believing they have the option to attend a school outside your state borders. Bruce Williams, radio Talk Net's financial advisor, cautions that if you purchase a California college bond, for example, and then you swarm outbound as soon as you can afford a U-Haul, there could be a question as to whether the child holding the bond is eligible for a California education, since he would no longer be a California resident at the time of enrollment in college.

The Zingeroo-22 is that if the youngster does not go to college, the bond is non-refundable and non-redeemable. A baccalaureate bond is a very, very cheap way to insure a college education . . . if everything goes right. It's like putting a quarter in the slot in Reno; if you come up with bars all across you've made a terrific investment.

The other catcheroo, in some states, is that you might well be concerned about your state's prospects of solvency by the time your kids' bonds mature.

Comparative costs, tuition and fees only, 1990:	
Public 2-year colleges:	$ 758
Public 4-year universities:	2,006
Private 2-year:	5,324
Private 4-year:	10,400
— World Almanac	

This is one hope we must cling to, and that is, in the words political speechwriters so oft repeat: This Can Not Stand. We would like to believe that America simply can not and will not allow education to price itself out of Americans' reach— although the cynic which has earned the right do dwell within us might sneer, "Why not? Housing and health are."

By now, you thirtyish-somethingers who couldn't wait to get out of the house, you can see the direction things are going. The old folks? You wouldn't believe how many of them say, "I hope the kids get into a house of their own by the time I have to move in with them. Life shall so soon become just. If my kids thought I was incompetent when I was thirty . . . . Oh, boy, wait till they see me at seventy-four."

That will happen about the same time *your* kids have grown up and come home. They'll probably bring one or two of your grandchildren. Now . . . why was it you couldn't wait to get a place of your own?

> The Crunch Generation: You haven't paid off your debts for college, but it's time to save for your kids'..
>
> You couldn't wait to get out of the house, but you had to move back.
>
> You haven't afforded a home, but you'll have to soon, so your folks can move in it when they're old.

14

Arguers

My thesaurus and dictionaries say "debate" and "argue" are synonyms. In everyday vernacular use, however, we differentiate, making the one an admired intellectual activity, the other a scorned personality disorder. Debate connotes a high level mental process, combining rhetoric with an armament of facts and supportive quotations. Argument has come to mean contrariness and obstinacy.

Kids are born arguers, and few things they do stir up as much parental snapback. Sometime around their second birthday, kids seem to run on auto-response: "But — " . . . "Why — " It wears us down, then we begin to respond back. As soon as we hear But and Why, we froth, like Pavlov's dogs when they heard the bell. Before he's two, we've grown confrontational by habit. It will continue through 8, 12, 15 . . . Forever.

Mother *(commanding)* : Get your junk off the sofa.

Child *(trying to explain):* But I —

Mother *(angry):* Don't argue with me!

Child *(defensive):* But I put it there so —

Mother: Don't use that tone on me. I won't have you mouthing off.

The boy gathers his books and backpack and takes them to his room. Mom is satisfied that she's curtailed an argument and nailed up another beam in the structure of respect and obedience. Youngster feels defeated, having been denied the opportunity to explain how he had solved a problem, one more proof that his initiative is invalid, his individuality not valued.

You see, in the morning flurry, the youngster sometimes couldn't find the things he was supposed to take to school, or he couldn't remember it all. So this evening he gathered it together and set it near the door. His attempt to explain was taken for argument. He was shut off, unlistened to.

Don't automatically assume that a child's response to an order is argument. Listen to what he says. Don't be so quick, either, to reprimand "that tone of voice." What you may be hearing is simply a *childish* voice. Sure, it's high pitched. Hear again: is he really whining, sassing, or talking back — or is he pleading to be listened to?

Whether they're 2, 10, or 17, kids argue for pretty much the same reasons. To verify the consistency of the rules. To assert that they are independently thinking beings; to confirm the validity of their opinions. Or just because it's a habit.

But let's admit it. There are the contrary ornery rasty buggers who argue to be disagreeable; who, if they continue, will become adults without redeeming values. Between the gut-reaction arguer and the cerebral debater the line is nearly imperceptible, at least until about 7 or 8. How do you tell which is which, and how do you nurture the one and squash the other?

When the child counters you, first let him finish what he's saying. Then ask him to tell you: Why do you want to . . . Why don't you want to . . . What do you think . . . What is your reason for . . . Why would it be better if . . . ? Phrase questions which require multi-syllable answers and some thought, like essay questions on a test.

Leading a youngster in this manner will accomplish many things.

You're listening. You're engaging in dialogue. You have to listen if you are to come back with appropriate questions, and he has to respond if he has a real point to make.

You compel the youngster to think. Your questioning forces him to analyze and rationalize, which is very different from merely reacting and shooting off. The difference between argument and debate.

You foster discussion, which means both of you must first intellectualize, then articulate your premises. Few youngsters are given enough opportunities to do this.

Gradually, the young person will come to realize that you can hash things out, and even disagree, without being confrontational. And that might be good for you, too, because you may have to be the first to learn how to talk without getting hostile.

On the other hand, if the kid's Why and Yeah-but does, in fact, come from contrariness, defensiveness, defiance, orneriness, or just plain habit, then you can blow your whistle and call the bluff. Ask some questions requiring logical answers or sensible options and you'll find out pretty fast if he's simply arguing for the love of argument. More important, he'll realize you've got his number. Beyond that, if you provide him with such a springboard, you will be launching that arguer on his way to becoming a thoughtful debater.

There still are times, however, when the right answer is "Because I said so."

It was in the cereal aisle of one of those six-acre warehouse discount markets. The store probably carried all the 131 new cereals marketed last year and the five hundred older brands besides. I turned the corner to see a pair of boys about 9 and 11, and their mother with a piled-high shopping cart.

"Well, actually . . . because I'm the adult here and I said so, that's why," the mother was saying, and she looked around to see if anyone had heard.

I thought about nodding to her, maybe even saying something like, "Sometimes that's exactly the right answer." But I didn't, because the mother's body language said that she already knew it was. The little boys knew it was too, because they had already gone dancing off elsewhere, chattering and chuckling.

So instead of speaking to her, I peeked into her cart to see what kind of cereal she had, because I wanted her brand. I put the Cheerios and Multi Bran Chex in my cart, a stockpile of good stuff to have on hand for the grandkids.

> Don't automatically assume all a kid's responses are argument. Ask questions requiring thoughtful answers, and listen to them. After that, remember there really are times when the correct answer is *Because I'm the adult here and I said so.*

15

Debaters

"He argues," a mother lamented. "Everything I say is answered But . . . but."

"He's intelligent," I told her. "He is able to see various views of everything, several solutions to a problem. He isn't arguing just for the love of arguing. In fact, he isn't arguing at all. He's debating aloud with himself, laying the issue out and looking at all its sides."

"It comes across as arguing, and it's difficult to live with." The mother sighed. "His dad's brothers are like that, and so are their daughters. If you say it's Tuesday, they'll argue it's Wednesday; they'll try to tell you black is white."

"That's not surprising, because Kevin's brand of debating comes from the ability to examine and analyze, and that aptitude is a genetic program that runs in families." I told her.

I had taught Kevin in nine different classes over the last four years, and in that time I had sort of figured out how his thinking system was wired. Like others who think in this program, Kevin could explain that Tuesday *is* Wednesday: Tuesday here, Wednesday across the date line; and that white *is* black: white absorbs all the colors; black, none. That the sum of two and two depends upon the binary system in reference.

But living with a highly analytical person can be difficult, and right now Kevin's mom needed empathy. I told her, "I know what you go through. My brother is like that, and my son; and yes, you're right: it isn't easy." Kevin's mom had found out what all her parents-in-kind eventually discover: It is infinitely more difficult to raise a brilliant child than a barely average one.

Many of those exasperating children who argue, who challenge every statement, every directive, do so because they operate on a particular intellectual plane — and a high one it is. Even though they put everyone around them through some awful times, their capacity should be celebrated . . . and

51

nurtured. If he is properly directed, the argumentive child can become the open-minded, fact-seeking, problem-solving adult; the individual who invents alternatives, who does not fear following his own compass, composing his own drumbeat. A cutter of edges.

Recognizing different views of the same picture, then analyzing, making judgments, and finally forming an opinion: those are the elements of debate. A debater makes decisions, then defends them; but the decisions are not based upon what's In.

In some forms of debate, an individual's point of view is more or less assigned. *My dad is the smartest dad in the world.* (If I had a different dad, *he* would be the smartest.) *Cheatslip High is Number One in America's Heartland.* (I wouldn't say that if I didn't go to Cheatslip.) *He's innocent.* (I am the Public Defender; of course he's innocent.) *Having lost the nomination, I will rally 'round the candidate, heal the wounds, and support the party.*

In formal debate in high school, students are assigned sides; one argues For or Against because the speech coach says he will. At a regional speech tournament, I adjudicated the Affirmative team of Goldman and Borth to be the winner of Debate 1. My decision was based upon the quantity, quality, and authoritative sources of the evidence they produced, and the conviction with which they presented it.

In Debate 2, the same question, the winner was the Negative team of Goldman and Borth.

"How do you *do* that?" I asked.

"Just doing our job," Borth said.

The person who can see every side of a question is able to weigh advantages and disadvantages, and also to pick out fact from fluff. Kevin, Goldman, and Borth will not be hornswaggled by advertisers, fooled by politicians, or duped into donating to fake charities. As teen-agers, they aren't swayed by peer pressure and not influenced by what all the other kids think. As adults, they won't succumb to mob psychology nor to opinions, behaviors, or prejudices only because they're socially correct.

Societies which value inquiry, analysis, and private and public argument are unlikely to fall for ideas like "holy wars" (the Crusades were waged not from religious conviction but from the nothing-to-boredom of a dull and peaceful feudal life); nor throw out its lepers, permit lynchings, or let Hitler happen.

For all that, a downside exists. (A good debater recognizes upsides and downsides.) Some persons are so highly analytical, so able to see every plus and minus of every angle that they wind up unable to make any decision at all. The purpose of collecting and weighing evidence is to expedite decision making, yes; but some individuals read so much into their information that the plusses and minuses balance out. Deadlock. No decision.

This kind of person is very intelligent; he has so much intelligence he stumbles on it. But in his moments of indecisiveness he seems quite dim.

"What kind of car are we going to get?"

"This one has these advantages and these disadvantages. That has these ups and these downs; and this one . . . I don't know; what do you think?"

"Let's get this one."

"But . . . but . . . how can you like that one . . . ?"

Sometimes, you'd like a nice quick, thoughtless snap decision. Sometimes, I know exactly how Kevin's mom feels.

The ability to ferret facts, to sift out the fluff and analyze what's left, is an intellectual prize. The person who does this will not succumb to polls, peers, or pressure. With enough people like this, anarchy can not happen.

16

PR and the school schedule

"The worst PR for the schools is the district's bleeping, fleeping schedule," rails an irate dad. "This is the third largest district in the state. Last November, school was in session nine days. They took off two holidays and another two days for teachers' in-service, where they get paid for eating doughnuts and listening to speeches which don't tell them anything new. Four more days for parent-teacher conferences — which they schedule for the same hours parents work, then they rail us for not being concerned enough to attend."

The local newspaper carried a half-page feature about the schools' schedule and the childcare conflict it created. For parents of pre-teens, it is always a monumental hustle to find places for kids to go when they don't go to school. An administrator whose status was stratospheric enough to entitle her to speak for the district responded this way: "The schools cannot make schedules around day care."

"The schools promote themselves as caring about kids, even about the welfare of the community," the dad continues railing. "And then they proclaim an official policy of not giving a rip about childcare."

In Seattle, teachers were on strike. Early Monday morning they turned out by the thousands, human trains and chains clogging freeway ramps, waving fists and yelling crudities at commuters. As if it were Joe Workingman's fault the teachers and the Legislature were at odds as to what constitutes a quality education.

"It isn't just their being so bleeping obnoxious," Joe Workingman said. "But they're such a scuzzy looking outfit. Ratty clothes, wild hair; even their placards are crudely lettered. Those are professionals? The paid role models for my kids?"

Across the continent, a Floridian said, "Our middle school of 500 students has three assistant principals. That's *asking* for lousy PR. Taxpayers are never likely to vote more funding for the necessities while there's an overload at the top. Especially when it is not clear just what all those administrators *do.*"

What the schools don't do to themselves, the kids do for them.

In a city on the east side of San Francisco Bay, a citizen complains: "You see kids wandering around any hour of any day, and you wonder why they aren't in school. You could give them the benefit of the doubt. Maybe they're homeschool kids; maybe they're on an educational field study. Naahh, not on bikes and skateboards, not in pairs hanging out at the mall. Besides, homestudy parents aren't the kind who let their kids run around loose during school hours."

Now that he's nicely warmed up, the Californian goes on. "We keep hearing the schools are overcrowded and they need more money for more of everything. The thing is, so many kids are out of classes on any given day that the classrooms are probably only half-full, anyway. It's hard to convince me I want to pay for more schools for kids to skip."

A teacher in a tough St. Louis neighborhood counters, "If a kid's on the street, it's one less confrontation at school."

What can a parent/citizen/taxpayer do? Can an individual make any difference?

In spite of what they told us in high school civics, the Real World answers are Not Much; and Not Likely.

Joe and Jane Workingperson are infinitely better informed than were citizens of prior generations, yet they find they have increasingly less influence. They're in an angst of helplessness and impotence, the feeling that *They* don't give a rip. And that, I think, is why Talk Radio has catapaulted to such enormous popularity, and why newspapers are giving ever more space to Letters to the Editor, and a computer network's Education Issues bulletin board is so busy.

Traditionally, the most obvious way for a citizen to make differences has been to serve on the local school board. "That doesn't work here," an elementary teacher in a Deep South city told me. "Our schools are entrenched in Good Old Boy machine politics, and the GOBs have effective ways of muffling unwanted voices."

The machine is precisely the reason so few citizens are willing to take on The System. As soon as a candidate files for a position on the nonpartisan, nonpolitical school board, he becomes a political figure by the mere virtue of being a candidate. "Filing for public office is like asking to have all your past files opened," a Washington man said. "I'd like to run for the school board, but if I do, some past-scraper will bring up my failed business of fifteen years ago." He adds, "If I weren't a party caucus chairman my past might be more insignificant."

A mother in a rural community served two terms on her local school board. "In a small town, an individual has a greater chance to make a difference, and I did," she said. Her board, at odds with The System then in place, toughened the curriculum and directed some policy changes. "Then the teachers got to taking it out on my kids," she said, "and that's when I quit."

We like to think teachers are above Taking It Out. They aren't. During Contract Dispute Time in a town in this valley, teachers picketed the pharmacy which employed a board member. "The ruckus is hurting my business," the owner told the teachers. "Please stop." The teachers did not.

In another city, striking teachers picketed the school buildings, urging kids and substitute teachers not to enter. On the local news we saw a teacher crying — *crying!* "The substitutes will ruin my students the subs can't possibly love them as I do it will take me the rest of the year to undo the damage the children will never regain the education they are losing."

Then why . . . ? Don't bother to ask.

In 1992, some teachers in New York state protested The System by putting in their time and nothing more. According to a teacher who did not participate in the sitdown, "They teach for 40 minutes per period and that's it. No class discussions, no questions taken. They won't check papers and they won't attend any school events. Their rooms are undecorated, bare and depressing."

For every strike and protest, there are those who don't agree and won't participate. "An entire staff of supposed professionals splits into factions. Our side against their side," said a Eugene, Oregon teacher who had been through it. "After ten years, the wounds still have not healed."

Perhaps we actually can do Not Much, and our making a difference is Not Likely. On the other hand, whatever we try can't flop any harder than everything else has.

The first premise is this: Bad PR isn't exclusive school property. It isn't all generated by the fat cats on the overpopulated top rung. There may be a little something each of us can do. As they say, with our combined strength and voices . . . you know, the stuff about drops filling the bucket.

❑ ADMINISTRATORS: Many school districts issue periodic newsletters to the populace. Good idea. But why fill it with fluff? I *expect* fifth graders to study mapping and I *expect* third graders to write storybooks.

Give me some hard stuff: What is it those five vice principals and 23 people in the central office *do?* Job descriptions, please, along with no-hype figures telling how many children each cat serves, in what ways. How many students are actually in the band you propose to cut, and how many in geometry and calculus? What exactly do teachers do at those in-services; who are their workshop presenters; and by what virtue do they know something your staff doesn't know already?

❑ TEACHERS ASSOCIATION: *Prove* to me you're underpaid. Give me some numbers. How much does each teacher cost? I want to know if the district's policy is to hire the cheapest, most inexperienced staff; or if it values seasoning and advanced degrees.

How much per hour are teachers paid; and how much per hour *per student?* If you really want to make a point, give the folks the figures that will show, once and for all, that the seventh grade teacher makes less per hour per child than parents pay the seventh graders to baby sit in the evening.

Combat pay, teachers? A lot of you deserve it. Got any facts and figures? Pick a week: How many come stoned, hung over, speeded up, or slowed down? How many knives do you see, how many times are you cursed at and punched out?

How many kids show up bruised, hungry, and otherwise abused and neglected? How many are responsible for feeding, washing, putting to bed and getting up younger siblings? In fact, what's the younger-sibling case load for some of your older students?

How many kids completed and handed in their assignments, and how many did not, in Algebra I/ World History/ Bookkeeping/ Whatever? What alibis, reasons, and excuses did you hear for not working and not showing up?

When you provide these hard facts, by the way, two or three of your constituents might even catch on that not every failure is *your* fault, which is pretty much the pillory you're on right now.

And stop the lobby about "Well, we have to keep taking classes at our own expense, you know." So do your carpet cleaner, your accountant, your newspaper reporter, your cablevision technician. In fact, in this age of technology and information, much of what we learned last year is already obsolete, and isn't it a teensy bit incongruous that the loudest complainers about having to get educated are educators?

And, please, if you do go on strike, think up a different slogan than "On Strike For Our Children."

❑ MIDDLING-TO-OLDER CITIZENS: Your kids are out of school and you no longer have a vested interest in public education. Really? Well, let's see: The persons you'll count on to advise you in managing your retirement funds, to assess the valuation of your property, fill your prescriptions, keep your car running and your roof plugged, to become your grandchildren's employers and mentors, and to staff the nursing home you'll enter — they're probably around junior high, high school now, don't you suppose?

❑ PARENTS: When you ask, "What did you do in school today?" and he answers, "Nothing," do you accept it at face value? Does he really have no homework, again? For that matter, do you know for a fact that he was *at* school, *in* classes?

Have you seen first hand, or heard a first-hand report from the school, that validates what your child tells you about being picked on, put down, or having too much expected of him? Do you know for sure whether he is giving you straight facts, or snow jobs?

As a last resort, try this little self-checker: How would it be if you had 37 of him in a room thirty feet square for six hours?

❑ CITIZENS: Write to school administrators and board members. Writing Letters to the Editor and calling Rush Limbaugh may temporarily temper your adrenaline, but editors and Rush cannot effect changes in your local schools. Administrators and board members can.

Express your concerns, ask questions, and offer solutions. Board members − those brave persons who offer themselves up to public scrutiny in order to make differences they believe in − stand a much greater chance of being effective if they have the support of their constituents. Or their non-support, if constituents can offer some viable, thoughtful alternatives. Preferably in writing.

Maybe we could shake The System if we joined up together and steamrollered 'em, like a snowball from Hell.

❑ STUDENTS: The product can never be better than its raw materials. If you want to make a silk purse you need a piece of silk. Changing everything but kids' behavior is like putting Band-Aids on a man who needs a bypass.

If First Communion, Confirmation, or Bar Mitzvah signal the advent of the age of reason, then the kids who hang the streets or, worse, take their attitude to school, have reached the age of reason; and that means they're running on their own generators.

And while we're about it, let's encourage the school to schedule its schedule around child care, and family life . . . little things like that which will make us believe they believe what they say they believe in.

17

Preschool: What, Why, How

By JENNY LAKEY

Jenny Lakey is president of the parents' group of Mulntnomah Preschool Cooperative, Portland, Oregon.

The November my son was two and a half, I sat on a folding chair at the indoor park and watched him on the slide. Climb up . . . swish down. A static charge on the slide made his hair stand up, making him look perpetually surprised, while his eyes smiled brightly as he delightedly found new ways to up-end himself on the thing. He comically illustrated the wonder of being a child.

One of the mothers sitting near me said, "So. Do you have Brian signed up for preschool yet?"

Preschool! Brian wasn't even potty-trained. His pre-school career was almost a year in the future. "No," I answered. "I was hoping to get Thanksgiving and Christmas safely discharged before tackling that one."

"Don't wait," she said. "You should get him on waiting lists right away." Waiting lists? "Yes," she continued. "This is when they start filling up."

I could scarcely believe I'd have to put that much effort into preschool. I proceeded to do nothing, then had virtually the same conversation with another woman the following week. Still I did nothing until January. Then from a county agency I got a list of preschools in my area.

I called the ten nearest schools, asked long lists of questions, and ranked them according to what I felt to be their merits. On all the waiting lists I ended up way down, sometimes number 50 or 60. Each registrar assured me I'd be called come August because, like me, everyone was on at least ten waiting lists, arbitrarily inflating the lists.

Several schools wanted to put my daughter on their waiting lists as well. "Katie? She's only six months old!" They proceeded to explain how many unborn children were already listed.

Preschool began to take on the look and feel of a commodity, something that increased in value according to its scarcity. Ironically, that seemed to devalue it, as though most parents were motivated by keeping-up-with-the-Joneses, making sure that Gregory and Meredith had the same early advantage as Jessica and Ryan, by George! As though what a child might miss by *not* going was as important as what he'd get by *going*.

Did parents I know really have something in mind for their kids, or did they casually accept preschool as a natural precursor to kindergarten and first grade? What exactly was the advantage of preschool? When I was a tot there were few preschools; not even many kindergartens. This doesn't appear to be a serious setback for my age group; so it can't be argued that preschool fills an educational vacuum.

I've come to see preschool as a social phenomenon, something that makes up in part for the increased isolation and fragmentation of families, and to some extent my experience bears that out. But my question still remained: What is the advantage of preschool?

To analyze that, I had to articulate my goals as a parent, and to determine how a preschool could help me accomplish them.

My overriding goal for my children is for them to be secure and independent. For them to become decision-makers, initiators, people who can deal with change and are able to take risks. They might ask my advice but not necessarily need it. They may not even need me. Their first steps toward independence, however . . . I want to share them.

I want my children to gain pro-social skills with agemates and adults, to learn what to do with their emotions, to assert, express, and accept themselves in socially acceptable manners.

In a preschool, I want a philosophy emphasizing social skills and emotional well-being more than academic learning. I strongly believe in the importance of learning through play.

I want a teacher who welcomes my input, responds to it, and respects my judgment. A good teacher knows more than I do about children in general — behavior, development, learning patterns. But I know my particular child better than anyone, and my observations can be quite valuable.

Finally, I found that school.

THE CO-OPERATIVE PRESCHOOL

Multnomah Co-operative Preschool is one of the best in Portland, with a remarkable teacher from whom I've learned much. Multnomah holds accreditation from the National Association for the Education of Young Children, a rarity for a preschool. The school stresses the "whole child" developmental approach, emphasizing socialization and emotional well-being over academics.

The school is run by parents and teacher working together. Parents work, actively and physically, on every phase of the school's operation, from maintaining the building to planning the curriculum to assisting in the classroom. I like the arrangement because it satisfies my need to work alongside other adults at the same time I share my child's first experiences away from home.

Most of all, the co-op reinforces the social skills my kids are beginning to learn. What better model than watching moms and dads working together at school, using the communication skills the children themselves are learning? For that matter, a lot of us parents are learning pro-social skills along with our kids. The school has the group feeling I want: the connection between parents and children, between school and home.

On a deeper level, Brian is learning that his parents are inside the learning process, part of it.

My school s parent-teacher conference exemplifies mutual respect and communication. Beforehand, parents write their observations in six categories of development: social, emotional, language, cognitive, gross and fine motor coordination, learning style/special interests. The teacher fills out an identical sheet. At the conference we compare notes.

Learning through play — Before I ever thought about preschool, before I ever thought about my children's education, I watched Mr. Rogers telling me how important play is. It seemed like both an old and a new idea at the same time. That kids need to play is an old idea; to analyze its benefits seemed new. I have read numerous articles in which experts analyze play, stress its importance, and encourage lots of it. Their ideas fall in line with my own instinctive feelings about the healthiness of play.

Each day, Linda, our preschool teacher, makes in-depth observations and records the activities and interactions of one or two of her children. This is Linda's record of one of Brian's days:

12/2 Excited! Spent long time in back room, active, a little wild, put goggles on, tried to scare peers. Altercation with Bobby who then scared him. Intervention needed. Brian moved on to carpentry, sawed paper towel rolls. Then back to more wild play. Finally went to dreidel game, PH [parent helper] said patient, sweet mood, counted carefully, enjoyed. On to stencils, worked hard, announced, "Mine is better than yours." Peers discussed this comment; he wore a frown. Focused easily during group time, seemed interested in discussion. On his way to wash hands spotted my placemat beside his, came and told me he read my name by his. At table much discussion about all kinds of sharks. Ate quickly, wanted more. Later went and told PH thank you for bringing snack. Outside played freeze tag. "Saved" peers, smiled, pro-social in his moves. Loved our made-up story, but when group got to decide what they would do in the story, made it clear he wouldn't get up at midnight to go investigate with the group.

What are some of the things Brian learned?
He found out that scaring people may cause them to scare back, that his behavior has an effect on other and sometimes has negative consequences. He learned more cause and effect when he worked at stencils and his playmates called him on a boastful comment.
He did some number play, showed confidence in his abilities by "reading" the teacher's name although he can't read;

and politely expressed great appreciation for the snack (which must have been sweet).

He got to contribute to a story with some other class-mates and at the end found it was okay not to follow the group.

My observations are a result of working with and learn-ing from Brian's teacher for the past two years, plus related reading I've done. A child professional could probably find even more. I'm pleased to see he experiments with different ways in approaching people, evidence of progress in socialization. I also note with satisfaction the great variety of his activities.

CHOOSING A SCHOOL

Preschool offers parents an advantage the public schools do not: We can choose our preschool. Certain characteristics define a good one. Below is a kind of checklist based on literature from Parent-Child Preschools of Oregon, to which I've added.

Teacher — First and foremost is the teacher. She or he sets the climate for the whole school, not just the classroom. Her permanence while an annually changing membership marches past gives her a strong voice in all matters; her approach to the members sets the tone and the degree of smoothness with which the school operates.

Look for a skilled manner in speaking to children — a quiet voice, a low posture at the child's level; giving directions telling them what *to* do, not what they *shouldn't* do; and providing alternatives to help solve problem situations.

Look for an accepting atmosphere where individual differences are are OK; where kids aren't pressured to complete this or that project. Notice whether the teacher allows children to express negative feelings as well as positive ones, and can guide them in handling them. Look for a classroom where parents are allowed to observe and be present until their new enrollee is comfortable.

Physical environment — Look for a setting that allows children to choose among activities, and which include those not requiring adult assistance. A stimulating environment should have areas for dramatic play, for manipulative toys, art activities and the supplies to carry them out. The room should be stocked with books, blocks, and a record or tape player, and places for each activities. And a playground.

The room should be bright and visually interesting. Furniture and equipment should be child-sized, child level. Also, note the ratio of adults to children.

Curriculum — A balanced preschool curriculum includes:

Speaking, listening, solving children's own problems, describing their feelings.

Creative expression through art, music, dramatic play.

Motor activities, fine (as stringing beads) and gross (large movements, as climbing, running, jumping), with time and equipment for each.

Experiences with cause-effect and predicting outcomes. (What do you think will happen when I add a stone to this full cup of water?)

Games involving numbers, counting, size, and quantity.

Concept development (facts and ideas) around themes (space exploration, the underwater world, the seasons).

Food preparation, cooking, experiments and experiences.

Field trips.

Schedule — Inquire about the daily schedule and times allotted to various developmental activities. A balanced day must include free choice time; play, both child-directed and teacher-directed. Large group activities and quiet, focused play. Robust physical action. Each day must inorporate variety.

Variety is the key. Kids need the big thrill of going to the fire station but also the quiet pleasure of feeding a bunny. They need to play house, make up stories, paint, dance, sing, spill things, drop things, pick up things. Push somebody, get pushed back, fall down, be comforted, comfort someone else. Jump, run, shout, laugh, and be quietly instrospective.

By these means kids learn about people and a world

filling quickly to the brim. That's knowledge they can't do without.

Fortunately, kids can play and learn at the same time. Parents, too, for that matter. We can show them the world, then delight in seeing it through their eyes. We can pass on the best of what we remember, and add some things we think we missed the first time. We are, after all, sharing the wonder.

I believe the experts who say the extra effort, time, and attention early on will come back with dividends later. I also believe my parents' affirmation of swiftly passing time. "Twelve years," my father says, "then they just want to do things with their own friends."

He pauses. "I'm 68 now. It might as well have been twelve days."

18

Advice to a new teacher

By VICKI JACOBSEN

Vicki Jacobsen teaches middle grades in an
inner city school on the Gulf Coast.

Remember that shiny, new, well equipped lab school where you did your student teaching? Well, try to put it out of your mind. Your new school won't come close in comparison. Positions at the "better" schools are prizes given those with seniority and connections. First you pay your dues.

Be prepared to spend several hundred of your own dollars the first few months of school. You have to supply your own cleaning materials, bug spray (roaches are abundant), air freshener (baths are infrequent); chalk, paper, pencils, pen, room decorations, tape, visual aids . . . and on and on. In fact, some schools provide you only with desks, chairs, textbooks and students. Sometimes there won't be enough desks, chairs, or texts. There will always be enough students.

Don't assume that students who are on grade level can do grade level work. Be prepared for first graders who don't know the alphabet and fourth graders who can't add two-digit numbers. Watch for students who have their names tattooed on their hands. They can't write their names, but they can copy them.

Don't try to break up a fight single-handedly and never try to disarm a student. Your life is worth more than your $18,000 salary.

Never come in contact with body fluids. Wash your hands frequently and keep plenty of disinfectant on hand. Lice, dysentery, pink eye, hepatitis, colds, and flu make the rounds. HIV cases are increasing rapidly.

Read everything you can find on Fetal Alcohol Syndrome and the effects of prenatal drug use.

Try not to cry when a pregnant fifth grader asks you how this happened to her. State law says you can't discuss sex until she's twelve.

Lock your purse in the trunk of your car every morning. Carry only enough money for the Coke machine. Don't wear expensive jewelry. Keep your classroom locked at all times, and never stay late unless you have a "buddy" who stays with you.

Find out what gangs operate in the area, their colors, signs, and enemies. Learn to recognize symptoms of drug use as well as drug paraphernalia. Never confront a student about gang affiliation or drugs. Notify the administrators and let them handle it.

Report all suspicions of abuse and neglect, but don't get upset if no action is taken. Child Welfare has ten times more cases than they can handle. Try not to get sick when you find dead roaches in a child's hair, black rotted stubs for teeth, and open sores.

Watch the news every night. The number of shootings in the neighborhood today will affect how your children will behave tomorrow.

Don't agonize over things you can't change. You have them only seven hours a day. The streets have them the rest of the time. You can't stop the bullets from flying, get Mama out of jail, or close down the crack houses.

Don't feel like a failure if you decide to give up. I read somewhere that 50 percent of all new teachers quit within five years. At least once a day, I wish I were one of them.

19

Family fun and hassle

Tuesday matinee at the Big Top. This one's at the Portland Coliseum; but it could have been the Kingdome or the Indiana State Fairgrounds. It's mostly grandparents and youngsters who pour into The All-American All-Star Three-Ring Second-Greatest Show on Earth (there's one born every day). At the beginning, everyone is festive and cheerful, high on anticipation.

In the middle, voices lift a pitch and temper-fuses sizzle. "Because I said so. You can't have everything you see."

At the end, the bigger children emerge sullen, the little ones crying, the grandmas and grandpas disillusioned and angry.

At the gate, moms and dads meet the old folks and kids, and the mothers ask brightly, "Did you have a good time?" and the little boys and girls cry harder and say, "No. They didn't buy me anything."

"Today will be special for them," the dad tells his wife. "I'm going to expose them to new experiences."

The dad takes his two pre-schoolers and the second grader to a petting farm, where the youngsters walk among deer and pygmy goats and peacocks and feed the animals peanuts from a bag. They go to a children's museum, where they put their hands on art media and scientific experiements, and the dad buys each child an artist's tool — colored pencils, a box of paints, a package of clay.

The dad recalls one of his favorite childhood places and takes his children there. It's a sprawling shop called Pet Camelot and it holds fascinations like exotic birds and fishes, reptiles, amphibians, and small, furry huggables.

Each child wants to buy a pet; but despite the wails and tears the dad remains steadfast. He placates them by purchasing a catnip mouse for the family feline. "But I didn't mean something for Flower," the middle child puckers up and pouts. "I meant something for me." The dad cheers them up at 31 Flavors.

When the family arrives home, the mother asks, "What did you do today?" The children answer: "We got peanuts and pencils and ice cream."

The highlights were not what they did but what they got.

"I knew we were in trouble as soon as we stepped inside the Coliseum," a circus-going grandparent said. "The entire foyer, wrapped around the building, was wall-to-wall Things For Sale. Tee shirts, stuffed toys, inflatables, flashlights, widgets, gadgets, and gimmicks, all at rip prices. This was neither culture nor entertainment, it was crass consumerism. The ticket price was no more than a cover charge for a flea market. I was seething before we ever got to the grandstand."

Worse yet, the circus people refused to allow Things For Sale to be a matter of family discipline. Throughout the performance, vendors stalked the stands. Again and again they returned to each section, usually addressing the children.

I do not fabricate, I do not exaggerate — these are the actual words the hucksters spoke to the children: "Ready to buy your pop corn/kewpie doll/flashlight/anything yet?" (Tactic: Get the kids to make the buying decisions.) "Aren't they going to buy you anything?" (Expose the old folks as cheapskates.) "Haven't you worn them down yet?" (Whassamatter, you kids weaklings? Aren't you in charge here or what?)

A mother told me, "I know I should provide the kids with experiences and opportunities. But every experience comes commercially packaged. What's supposed to be enriching winds up being a materialistic battle."

Another parent said, "There are no cultural or educational experiences out there that are worth the emotional and financial anguish. Even the symphony sells stuff out front."

Adults-in-charge don't all agree as to *why* kids become materialistic. Some distraught parents lament, "He's *so much* like his dad/grandmother/my husband's sister." (The people he's so much like are always on the *other* parent's side of the family.) So far, we don't know for certain, but perhaps some of the I Want is built in; else how to explain that one child tours a store and enjoys *looking*, while the sibling wants to own everything in sight?

Some people believe TV commercials have created material kids; some say it's agemate pressure; and others insist that kids are merely following adults' examples.

Whether it's inborn or culturally induced, the State of I Want is tough to control, hard to eradicate once it's taken hold, and turns every place you go into a field of battle. Try the following.

❑ Study TV commercials with your kids. All right, brainwash them. If you don't, the hucksters will.

Teach your children the truth of advertising: It is intended to establish a desire for things you don't need, to create a market where there is none, and to play on the insecure, the indecisive, the social statusers, and the gullible. As you watch, let your cynicism show! "They tell you this cereal tastes good; they don't tell you it is not good for you." — "Why would I buy that car? I don't drive 110 miles an hour through jungles."

By the time they're seven or eight, children can understand "We can't afford it." Instill in them that there's no disgrace in not affording it; in fact, it's a value they may as well learn early.

❑ Take young materialists into stores only if you have to. There are times you must, especially if you're a single parent. But when you do, institute some hard-and-fast policies:

Discuss beforehand what items you will buy. Make it clear to the youngster that's *all* you're buying. Tell him you will not purchase his impulses so don't ask. Then don't.

When you see something you'd like to buy for the child, or something she "really wants," resist getting it then and there. Go back later, present it to her another day, but don't make it a reward for fussing about it.

Set an example by curbing your own impulses. If you

didn't discuss getting those earrings for yourself, don't buy them just now. You cannot cater to *your* I Wants and deny his.

❑ For a month or two, or all spring and summer if that's what it takes, offer your I Want only those experiences which are free; take him to places which have no Things For Sale, no machines to take your quarters. Your purpose is to break habits. Remove temptations and you remove the hassles.

Your local library and the city park are excellent Free Places. State parks, forests with hiking trails, the banks of rivers and creeks are unlikely to have salesmen hiding in ambush.

Other places where you can look but not buy: Museums of all kinds; art galleries; concerts in the park (there will be popcorn and drink vendors; set your parameters before you go). Art and craft shows can be lively and enriching, but I Wants need to understand beforehand that it's look-and-enjoy, not see-and-buy.

The same for antique shops, and everyone keep your hands in your pockets.

❑ While you travel home from any expedition, help kids of all ages verbalize what they did. This focuses upon what was done, seen, and learned; it reiterates and solidifies impressions; it places the importance on activities rather on material gains. You can further emphasize skills in language, organization, and memory by having school-agers make lists when they get home.

It is a great misfortune of our society that almost all the Fun For The Whole Family events are wars waiting to be waged. The county fair should be an enrichment experience, but you never get past the midway. A harvest festival is planned as Entertainment for All, but it's a landmine of consumer booby traps. The zoo becomes a battleground of where to go first and what to buy next. And they leave the circus in tears.

A business man set up a booth at his state's Biggest Annual Festival, the one which tallies 3 million revelers per year. It was a war zone the entire ten days, he told me. Two million kids begged, screamed, and cried for things, and a million parents yelled, smacked, and spanked.

"I never saw such child abuse," he said. "I'll never again go to a Family Fun Event."

Consumerism turns every "rich experience" into a family battle. You can retrain material kids. Educate them in consumerism. Set examples. Set limits, and stick to them.

20

Armchair psychology

"He's that way because when he was a kid he had everything handed him on a silver plate," the Old Wife said of a 30-year-old.

"Baloney," scoffed the second Old Wife, who knew him when he was a kid. "His childhood was quite sparse; that's why he's that way."

The child was throwing a tantrum in the store. "Well, I bet *she's* used to getting anything she wants," cynicized an onlooker.

"I bet she doesn't get anything at all. Kids are like that because they don't get enough attention," countered another. "She needs more quality time at home."

"What she needs is more quality smacks on the bottom."

"You can sure tell *he's* an only child."

"No, he's one of four."

"Well, he must be the spoiled baby. Probably has three older sisters who fawn over him and mother him, and his dad finally got a son and pampers the daylights out of him."

"Actually, he's the third. The birth order is girl, boy, boy — that's him — girl."

"Well, you can sure tell he's a child in the middle. Has to be rambunctious to get noticed. Wants everything because he has to take hand-me-downs at home and then give it up to the next one."

"He's that way because that's the way he is. He was active before he was born and he's been active ever since."

"That girl is so thin she must be anorexic. You can tell she's insecure and has no self-esteem."

"That child is too chubby. One look at him and you can tell he's insecure and has no self-esteem."

"Well, I'm kind of hefty, too, but my self-esteem is fine. I simply happen to like the taste of chocolate."

"Look at this child's drawing. All that scribbling, and those primitive dark figures. He must be hurt, angry or disturbed."

"You're looking at the drawing of a four-year-old. Actually, it's pretty advanced for his age."

Teacher: She's inherently bright and capable, but she's inordinately hesitant in approaching new tasks, reluctant to venture answers and to speculate in unfamiliar realms, and uncertain about solutions to problem-solving presentations, because she seeks perfection and accuracy and she is burdened with an intrinsic fear of failure. She must be gently guided, generously encouraged, and we must allow her to proceed at her own pace and according to her own level of confidence.

Dad: Nonsense. She's inherently sloppy and intrinsically lazy. You've been snookered.

"Teenagers are that way because . . . their mothers work, their mothers don't work; their parents are too lax, too strict, they ignore them, they overprotect them. It's because of . . . TV/ rap 'n' rock/ society/ the schools/ the decline of the family/ too much poverty/ too much affluence/ the turn away from religious values."

"None of the above. Teenagers are old enough to make choices. They are that way because that's the way they have chosen to be."

Everyone is an armchair psychologist. We all know a few basic theories of human behavior, and we try to apply them to every person, every setting. *He's like that because of this.*

Somewhere, you can find a theory to prove any notion. For every human behavior there is a wide choice of conflicting explanations — you can pick the one that fits.

Within the past ten years, we've taken giant strides in our understanding of human learning and behavior. We have added volumes and megabytes to our knowledge of the how-comes and what-thens. Unfortunately, millions of those armchair psychologists still work with theories they learned decades ago and haven't updated since. Consequently, when the Old Wives analyze *your* children, they are doing it with very old information.

But even those who know the most can seldom be absolutely certain about what makes each of us as we are. The causes and effects of human behavior have as many variables as there are people. We simply can not know that "Johnny does this because of that."

You might as well accept it: people are going to psychoanalyze your children, whether they know anything about your kids or not. If you participate in the process, however, you can help those Monday morning psychologists avoid errors and mis-labels. When you discuss your child's school life with his teachers, provide your own insights and information. It may be crucial to his academic progress and his lifelong social attitudes for you and the teacher to figure out together whether the kid is a sensitive perfectionist with a deep fear of failure, or a sly manipulator.

This doesn't mean you need to track down everyone you know, and the parents of all your kids' friends, to explain why he plays his particular drumbeat. Hit the important ones, the ones most likely to criticize your kids *and* your parenting: teachers and grandmothers.

Of course, you can't explain what you don't know. This means that first you'll have to do some careful analysis of your own. And when you do, you'll find yourself figuring out two people. Your offspring, and yourself.

> Everyone pretends to know, but no one *really* knows, why anyone is the way he is. Don't bet your kid's life on what strangers think.

3

Growing and Learning

Strong stems

21

Your job, our job

Enrolling a child in kindergarten is different now than it was in yesteryear. Then, a parent checked in at the school office and gave out some information. Okay, filled out a form. Child's name, date of birth. Check-mark innoculations the child had received and when; check-mark the childhood diseases he had already had. Parents' name, address, phone number, and ditto for "whom to contact in case of emergency."

In an earlier era, the "emergency" it was in case of meant in case he got sick enough to throw up: where would the school take him? In bygone times, schools didn't call someone to please come pick up a sick child; they made deliveries. In those days, they didn't get sued for making deliveries.

In return, the mom received another form: school supplies. Crayons, glue, blunt nosed scissors, things like that. How much milk money: a dime, quarter, or gold piece, depending upon which decade it was. And a spare pair of underpants to put on deposit, another "just in case."

Now, before the first day of school, kindergarten teachers schedule parent conferences. (Listen: kindergarten and first grade teachers are the educators most likely to devote free, unpaid extra hours to kids *and* to parents.) It's still mostly the moms who come, as it's been forever; but now, more and more dads are showing up, too, and their active involvement is a big plus-positive for kids, schools, and the dads.

The mother of a kindergartener-to-be had just attended the preschool meeting. The little boy couldn't have been more excited than his mom about this milestone in both their lives.

By the mom's report, the teacher began by explaining what five-year-olds are like. (If you think this seems like explaining Catholicism to a priest, you'd be surprised to know how many adults don't really understand what children are like.) She told the parents what kindergarten is, what it does, how it is done, and what it aims to accomplish.

"We need your help. We need your involvement," she said. "We can not carry out this crucial task alone."

"Okay, I can conduct lessons at home," the kindergarten mom said. "I can help him with his math and reading. I've already taught him letters, numbers, colors, and how to tie his shoes."

I think that what the teachers really mean is that they can do *their* job only if parents do *theirs.* I think they meant the parents' job is to see to it that the child is cared about, that his health needs are met, that he is well nourished, and rested. That he is cared about, emotionally stable, and has a liberal measure of self-esteem. That he is cared about, interacts well with others, recognizes a world outside of himself, and behaves within socially acceptable parameters. That he is cared about, he counts, and he knows it.

If children bring with them these assets, these attributes which are fostered in the home and acquired much earlier than age five — or else, most likely, never acquired at all — then parents are, in fact, helping. Involved.

"I'm lucky she's my boy's first teacher," the mom said. A waitress at a good place just off Interstate 5, she spoke as she refilled cups at the counter. "I read that book about learning everything in kindergarten (Robert Fulghum's *All I Really Need to Know I Learned in Kindergarten*). Take turns, get along with others, clean up your own messes, wash your hands after the bathroom. But he's wrong about one thing."

She came to me, locked eyes, and I nodded. She freshened my cup and, without breaking pace, she continued. "Kids need to know those things long before they're five. Kindergarten is too late."

I am quite sure about what kind of help the kindergarten teacher meant. *If you take care of the physical, emotional, and social child, we can take care of the academics.*

I'm not so sure the mom caught that specific message, but I am sure she understands the principles behind it, and that she applies them. The teacher is lucky, too.

22

Enrolling in the bureau

Days, weeks before your child crosses the schoolhouse threshold, the Front Office hands you a bundle of papers. Homework already. "Fill out this form," she tells you. "Fill in the blanks." So which is it — Fill *Out*, or Fill *In?* Right away you start trepidating. If the honchess in the office can't tell Out from In, is this school in trouble or what?

This is more than your child's School Enrollment Form. It's her Big Brother Papers. You are enrolling her in the bureaucracy.

Child's Name Jennifer Ashley (or David Michael)
Sex _____

What do say about a five-year-old's sex? "Not yet"? . . . Oh, *Gender* — they mean What Is Your Child's Gender. Well, for heaven's sake, what gender do they think a Jennifer is?

You have to remember that this form was probably designed by a person born in an era when babies were given names like Pineleaf or Moonglow, or perhaps it was Tlung Tu, and nobody could tell whether those were boy names or girl names. Pine and Tlung got really weary of hearing, "Is that a boy name, or a girl name?," so they put a fill-in on the form.

Protected by the Right To Privacy Act, you opt not to fill the blank. These days it isn't required to reveal gender, since everyone has equal rights to wrestle, play trombone, or be a nurse. By the time your kid is 15, s/he won't tell, either, so you decide not to blow his/her cover.

Child's Social Security Number: ——— —— ———

The rule is: Every child must have an SSN to be enrolled in school. So hopefully you have Jen's/Dave's card in a safe place and the number in your wallet. Some parents delay getting that SSN "to keep my kids out of the bureaucracy for as long as possible."

"The Social Security Number will be your child's permanent personal identification," Office Honchess tells you. A necessity if one is ever to get a paycheck, savings bonds from the grandparents, to vote, or to get your grades from college, in case you want to see them. In fact, they don't even enroll you in college by name; you're filed numerically by SSN, and the numbers are gender-free, by the way.

You have serious misgivings about capriciously handing out your Big Bro No., because you know your every move can be tracked by following the footprints of your SSN. The people in the credit office at Mervyn's demand to know your SSN even though it is illegal to require customers to give it: "It's just our policy," they say. You are tempted to retort that shoplifting is illegal, too, but you'd like to make it your policy.

So if that number is so identifying, why don't they use it for my driver's license, library card, voter registration number and . . . and . . . ?

The mom on your right, the one wearing a scarf tied under her chin and a shawl around her shoulders, looks perplexed and glances at your paper. "You can leave blanks?" She speaks with an accent. "Okay, I'll tell them my Kqwrqtlaa is a boy and leave out Social Security."

You decide the real purpose of the SSN item is to track down people without Green Cards.

Religious Preference _____

You exercise your Right To Privacy again. The school's only possible reason to ask this, you guess, is so they'll know what kind of clergy to call if there's a stabbing on the schoolground.

Mother's Maiden Name _____

"That's just an additional identification," they explain. "In case we have two students named, like, Johnny Smith, we can easily tell which one is whom."

You challenge, "But you already have the Social Security Number. They tell me that's the only fact you need to pinpoint anyone." You resist adding, "All Sears has is my phone number, and they know all this stuff about me without having to ask."

The mom on your left says, "Your Mother's Maiden Name is the secret password, a security code for the child. If someone comes to the school and says, 'I'm Jennifer's cousin/uncle/ neighbor and I'm supposed to pick her up.' The school says 'What's Jennifer's mother's maiden name?' And let me tell you — some day you could be mighty glad the school has that secret word."

Another mom mumbles as she fills in the blanks:

Mother's Maiden Name   <u>Marinkovitch</u>
Paternal Grandmother's Maiden Name   <u>Leaping Deer</u>

Now another light dawns. They can get information about your child without asking direct questions. You provide a couple of facts, and Big Bro will make up the rest.

"Hey, don't worry about this stuff; they never use it," the mom on your left assures you. "Every time they want to know something, they call and ask. So I go, 'Why do you call me? You've got all this on file.' And they go, 'Oh, those files are too hard to find, we never use them.' "

"Sure, they do," says the former Miss Marinkovitch. "They sell your phone number to all those siding salesmen."

> So you wonder, "Is this my kid's pathway to education, or the paper trail to Big Brotherhood?"

23

The horror of hunger

Possibly the most appalling fact of contemporary America is that children are hungry. At least one in eight, perhaps as many as one-fifth of them, according to reports released in the spring of 1992. This does not mean the kids who fill up on junk food. It means *hungry*.

When a growing body is deprived of proper nutrition for very long, damage occurs. Much of the damage is irreparable. A generation of starved children will become a generation of dysfunctional adults.

If that terminology is too gentle, let me state it the way it really is: Starvation destroys brain cells. Destroyed cells are not regenerated. Starved children become mentally retarded adults. That is the horror of hunger.

Many argue that the earth is capable of producing sufficient food for all its inhabitants and a billion more. The problems, they maintain, lie in economics and politics. It is pretty generally known, for example, that during the Ethiopian famine in the 1980s there was food in Ethiopia. Millions of tons of food. Donated by people around the world. Stacked and rotting on the docks.

Most of the food did not get distributed to the starving. One, because the Ethiopian government denied there was a famine; it's bad politics to have people starving when your party is in power. Two, because the transportation system was so undeveloped it was next to impossible to move the food from dockside to countryside.

At the same time there were also new and renewed reports of poverty and hunger in America. I then lived in the lowest per-capita income county in the United States. Few of my students considered themselves *poor*. In fact, more than once, the teenagers engaged in fund-raising "for the poor." I never told them they were poorer than the poor they wanted to endow. There are various ways to measure riches.

One day, as we discussed the news of the world, a student who earned a respectable income as a summertime commercial fisherman offered his solution to the hunger problem. "Why don't the farmers send food to the poor?" He didn't use the words *humanitarian aid,* but that was what he meant.

"Do you mean donate part of their crops? For free?"

"Yeah," he said, and his classmates murmured their agreement.

"As commercial fishermen, you and your families are food producers, too, as surely as farmers are," I told the kids. "Would you give away part of your season's catch? No payment. Just give it away."

No, they wouldn't. For the first time, they looked at it as a problem they wouldn't be willing to help solve if they were asked to; and for the first time they began to grasp the dimensions of hunger.

There are many reasons for hunger, and not all of them are reasons of crop failures, economics, or politics.

After the formation of the Commonwealth of Independent States, bread all but disappeared from Russian stores. On Public Broadcasting's *Washington Week in Review,* journalist Hedrick Smith explained the bread shortage. Smith spent many years in the old Soviet Union, but not as a politician and not as a, quote, diplomat. He knows the people of Russia and Georgia and Lithuania and Armenia and all the others, as persons.

"To understand the shortage of bread in Russia," Smith said, "you have to understand the Russians." Each day, a store orders x amount of bread from the bakery. At day's end, the store returns all its unsold bread. But the bakery charges a return fee that is more than the bread cost in the first place. Therefore, to avoid losing money, stores purposely order short.

Russian bakeries have the capacity to produce enough bread for all, Smith said. But stores will not risk ordering "enough."

"Why the daily return?" a Washington Week panelist asked Hedrick Smith.

"That's what you have to understand about the Russians. They like fresh bread. They don't eat day old."

Bread shortage in the CIS? Self-induced hunger? It gives you something to think about, if you're an American family who buys at the Four-Day-Old-For-Half-Price shop while your government sends cash to people who won't eat it unless it's fresh.

I taught in seven towns in two states. A large majority of my students came from families representing the lower and lower middle economic strata. On a scale of One To Five, my kids would be Ones and Twos, with a minority of Low Threes. I never saw a correlation between hunger and economic status. The correlation is in the dedication of the adults the children live with; or, if we're still turning in gentle words for truthful ones, it's adults' *ambition*.

While you couldn't say they are actually well nourished, most older kids show up for school free of gnawing pain. Their younger siblings come hungry. The big kids' teachers say the big kids simply are better able to scrabble for what food there is. The other reason is that when an astounding number of little ones set out for school, "Mama and Daddy are still asleep." Six-year-olds tend to eat a better breakfast when someone gets up to pour the breakfast out of the box.

A second grade teacher communicated her concern to the parents of a child who every day arrived late, hungry, and unlaundered, and who every day missed both snack and reading time. The child's adult brother sent a scorching reply (the parents did not write) about sticking noses into people's lives. To explain it in gentler words than the brother used, a woodstove heats the house; the fire goes out during the night; it is too cold in the morning to get up. The logic was extended to justify not feeding the kids.

In another town, the parents of a first grader did not feed their little boy, period. They allowed him the handful of rice per day, except that in this case it was literal, not figurative. It was said around town that when the family ate its meals, little Ronnie was forced to sit in a corner and look but not touch.

The teachers stoked the boy almost continually while he was at school. He began picking up some weight and some color, and that's when his parents found out. His mother sent this note via Ronnie's eldest sister:

"Do not let Ronnie eat at school. When he come home he pee and all."

If the child had to go to the bathroom, it meant he was eating too much.

When nurses and social workers visited the town, Ronnie's mother always told the same story: "We don't have food." The boy's dad was perhaps the most notorious local shiftless; but the generous townspeople saw to it the family had more than enough food. Nearly always, their sagging porch was piled high with fish, game birds, rabbits. All of it a rotting, stinking stench. In truth, the family had fare fit for royalty, but nobody bothered to clean and cook it.

There are a lot of things we common-ordinary citizens-living-our-own-lives can do nothing about. Weather, economics, distribution systems, politics. But perhaps some of the horrors of hunger are of people's own making. As she watched the grade schoolers devouring lunch one day, one of my seniors commented, "Nobody in this town is without food. I wonder why so many little kids are so hungry."

> Starved children become mentally deficient adults. That is the horror of hunger. Many hungry children do not need to be. That is the horror of hunger.

24

Food for thoughts

Everyone knows children need food to grow. But we are ever more certain that nutrition is responsible for a lot more than simply increasing stature. Diet is a primary contributor to a child's behavior and intellectual development as well.

At a Portland, Oregon conference on early childhood, Gail Christopher, former executive director of the National Family Resource Coalition, presented a comprehensive report of a nutritional program implemented in Chicago. In the late 1980s Chicago's Head Start compiled data about Head Starters' health and socioeconomics, as well as a wide range of developmental factors — intellectual, social, emotional; language, motor skills, co-ordination, sleep patterns, behavior. After devising a baseline — the way it was before the project — Chicago instituted an intensive-care nutritional program for young children. Breakfast, lunch, nutritional snacks, vitamin supplements.

Positive improvement were measurable in one month. In three months, every child in the program had made demonstrable gains in every category. Within half a year, the changes in children stunned even the designers of the project. Children identified as behavioral problems, emotionally disordered, and intellectually disabled progressed to the margin of normal. In six months.

There are scores and hundreds of similar nutritional successes both on the record (written records, statistics, and reports) and off (observed but not necessarily reported, published, and put in a file folder in someone's office).

In 1982 one of my schools began serving breakfast to any and all students who came. Within days, teachers spoke of positive, even quite dramatic changes. The youngest kids apparently made the most gains, and our theory was that the small ones were less able to get up in the morning and get themselves something to eat. Or perhaps less able to scrabble for what food was on hand.

In one of my high schools a substantial percentage of kids showed up in the mornings fuzzy and grumpy. The most notorious grouch was a freshman who brought candy and pop and snacked her way through first period. (Yeah, I let them eat and they let me drink coffee. Okay, say I ran a loose ship. When your school has 38 kids and two teachers you can afford to operate more like a big family than like an institution.) All Marletta's sugar fix seemed to do was make her snarlier than ever.

Then came lunch. She put away a *l-o-t!* of food. And afternoons she was fine. . . . No, she underwent total metomorphosis. Smiling, sociable . . . she even learned a little in her afternoon classes.

"She's hypoglycemic," my colleague and I diagnosed.

It was 1978, and hypoglycemia was the buzzthing. It means the level of blood sugar is extraordinarily low. In terms of blood-and-brain chemistry, it's the same as a hangover. Conditions of body chemistry tend to be genetically influenced, and in our community: (A) most of the kids were cousins of some sort; and (B) few of them ate breakfast. So what we had was basically a high school full of hangovers. Big happy family notwithstanding, it was not conducive to morning comraderie.

My colleague and I prepared our case, then took it to the principal. Our record books showed that every single student got better grades in the afternoon than in the morning. More than that, nearly all the disruptions and discipline problems occurred before lunch. We were absolutely convinced there was a direct correlation between protein and carbohydrates in the stomach and failure and fighting in the classroom.

We agreed that every two weeks we'd switch the day. Afternoon classes in the morning. It didn't help the kids' dispositions, but it did boost half their grades. The following year, the school began a breakfast program and the morning terror was ameliorated.

"She's fine when I pick her up at the sitter's, but when we get home she cries and throws fits," a working mom told her aunt. "Do you think she doesn't want to come home?"

"I think she's hungry," said the aunt, who's a kindergarten teacher. "Does the sitter give them afternoon snacks?"

"She says she doesn't want to spoil their dinner. She doesn't feed them after nap time."

"Carry some bananas or apples or bagels in the car," said the friend. "Let her eat on the way home."

"I don't allow eating in the car."

The aunt's ancient station wagon had grown up six children. "Let them eat in the car," she said. "You can fix a messed-up car. You can't fix a kid."

One of the services of Child Care Information Services, a Community Action Program, is the training of child care providers. Their instructions: Don't let children go more than two hours without food. Meals, plus snacks. For pre-schoolers, a household rule of No Eating Between Meals is exactly the wrong one.

The information we are fed about nutrition, so to speak, is one of the facts of our daily lives that changes the most the fastest. (That and what's taxable this year and what isn't.)

In the olden days, there was The Basic Seven Food Groups and one of the groups was fat. We grew up calling pasta, rice, and potatoes "starch" and Starch had a bad reputation. Then Starch changed its name to Complex Carbohydrates, and now it's very respectable indeed — it should be 50 percent of your diet. We used to lament school lunches because they were "all that starch," and now we are told all that starch is the right thing to do.

We've also discovered that, instead of being a top-rated premium fuel, a high-protein breakfast slows you down — so that lowly bowl of oatmeal is the right thing to do, too. We once thought we did our families a big favor to send them off with bacon and eggs, and now we've found out that's how to kill someone you love. And the college kids' standby of Ramen noodles is a better breakfast than over-easies and hashbrowns.

Despite some dissonances about adults' diets (like whether or not coffee is bad) (don't let 'em take your quality of life away!) pediatricians and nutritionists are all in very close harmony about children's nutrition. The simple, no-fooling-around, easy-memory basics given here come from National Parenting Center experts Dr. Barton Schmitt of Children's Hospital, Denver; pediatrician Dr. Alvin Eden; and psychologist Vicki Lansky.

DAILY DIET
    ❑ 20 percent of calories from milk, meat, and eggs; 80 percent from fruits, vegetables, and grains (complex carbohydrates).
    ❑ One serving of meat, fish, or poultry per day is adequate; 2 servings maximum. (Other experts recommend more protein than that for pre-schoolers and adolescents. Perhaps this is one of those Take-Your-Choice items.)
    ❑ Eggs: Limit to 3 to 4 per week, including eggs used in cooking.
    ❑ After the child's second birthday, switch to 2% milk.
    ❑ Start the day with fruit juice, serve fruit or fruit juice every meal; fruit for dessert and snacks. (Note: Beverages labeled "Juice Drink" are NOT nutritionally equivalent to fruit juices.)
    ❑ Include foods high in fiber (whole grains, legumes, dried fruits, cabbage family, sweet spuds, raw produce).
    ❑ Include foods high in iron. (Easy-memory rule: If it's green, dried, or contains red blood, it's iron.)

TO CUT OR AVOID
    ❑ Fat
    ❑ Salt
    ❑ Refined sugar ("Sugar" sugar, as distinguished from sugars occurring naturally in fruits and starches. Honey is . . . sugar.)
    ❑ Smoked and/or cured meats. Bacon, ham, jerky, hot dogs, sausages limited to once a week treats.
    ❑ Chocolate *(Hey! Don't fire! I only report the news, I don't make it up.)*

It's one of our unfortunate paradoxes that the food that's baddest for us is also the most convenient and least expensive.

When you're on the run, you can grab a candy bar and put the wrapper in your pocket; but what do you do with an apple core or banana peel? You can fill up on a couple of doughnuts for sixty cents or a turkey breast on rye for $2.79.

Recently I called my kid in grad school. "Son, are you eating right?"

"Yeah, I guess so. I fill up on Top Ramen and take prenatal vitamins."

I also called my sister, an R.N. whose favorite duty is pediatrics. "Okay, we know what's good for us. Fresh fish, $6.99 a pound; broccoli at a buck. What do you eat at your house?"

"When this nest was full, we never skimped on nutrition. I've seen the results of sound diets and poor; and I'll tell you it is just simply absolutely totally not worth it to not nourish your kids."

My sister chuckled. "Some experts believe diet is more important to us empty-nest postpartums now than when we were thirty. You get to the place in your life where you can afford steak and fine cheese at exactly the time when you'd better go back to brown rice and beans."

"So what do you old guys eat?" I pressed.

"We don't do much ceremonial cooking here any more. Top Ramen and vitamins, and Tums. I'm not sure if the Tums is for John's cooking or for my bones."

> The most important ingredients for academic success are nutrition, language, and self-esteem.

25

What is it? How much does it take?

When he was attempting to justify cutting federal spending for school lunch programs, a well known United States president explained, "Ketchup is a vegetable." This gives us a whole new definition of fruits and veggies, and that's a big break for moms having trouble getting kids and men to eat what's good for them.

If ketchup/catsup is a veggie, then salsa, relish, pickles, and Kettle Chips must be, too; and jam, popsickles and lemon tea must be fruits. Now I can call my three-olive Martini a health food.

The new USDA guidelines come with a recommended number of servings for each food group. But it's a bit difficult to keep track of how many servings of what because you can't always be certain what to call the serving. Canned vegetable beef soup is likely to contain more barley than meat and veges. The ingredients of your homemade Saturday soup vary from Saturday to Saturday, and besides that, each person picks out different goodies from the pot.

What USDA recommends is . . . a LOT of food. Two dairy items isn't much, unless you're allergic to dairy products. Three proteins is manageable, too, except that some dieticians would like to reclassify peanut butter as a fat. But five fruits and vegetables minimum, with the accent on FRESH, is not only a plate full, it's spendy.

And get this: ELEVEN servings of the bread-cereal-rice-pasta group. So you may as well go ahead and eat your five bowls of Grape Nuts to get the same nutrition as one bowl of Total.

26

PB b/bag

Everyone has occasion to pack a brown bag.

"Bag" ranges anywhere from a four-courser in an insulated designer carrier, to a Cup O Noodles in case you can find hot water, to a sandwich stuffed into a purse or an apple rolling around the dashboard of the car.

The food section of a mega metro daily carried a big technicolor spread on bag lunches. From the article you could tell two things about the food writer: she buys her lunches out, and she never had kids.

Everyone knows that seventy percent of those bags contains a peanut butter sandwich, but the article's purpose was to convince metro sophisticates they wanted alternatives to the monotonous daily PBS. Now, any dedicated goober spreader might ruffle if you called their savored fare boring; and besides, why change it if we like it. We don't *want* alternatives to daily delights like showers, morning coffee, evening news, and PB sans.

In full living color was depicted the writer's preferred substitute for Dr. Carver's life work: a tomato-cucumber-cheese-alfalfa sandwich. On your choice of rye or pumpernickel, naturally.

"Bob, what would you do with that epicurean irresistible?" I asked the father of my children. "If you were a school boy again?"

"Trade it for a peanut butter sandwich."

"No, you wouldn't. Who'd trade with you?"

If you're into packing lunches often, spend Saturday morning making tomato and sprout sandwiches and freezing them, wrote the writer. But don't add tomatoes and sprouts to the T & S San until eat-em-up time, since they don't freeze well. Oh. I guess that's like the powdered water my sister gave us for our hiking trip. Anyway, if you made all your sandwiches on Saturday, what will you do with Tuesday night's meat loaf?

Wrap the freezer-ready morsels first in plastic, then foil, the item helpfully hints. Come on, girls; with the prices of shrinkwraps, you're doubling the cost of lunch before it ever hits the sack.

Cost? Will you really send the kids to school with tomatoes in December?

"More nutritious than PB," says the writer, "are cheese, meat, eggs." Nutritious? All that fat and cholesterol? If you mean protein, check your *The New Pocket Nutrition Edition*: PB beats all the above. So does the price.

That peanut butter sandwiches are liked by men and children is certainly a virtue, but their real advantage is their durability. A PBS can be left a whole weekend in a desk or the trunk of a car and not turn furry. They can be stacked on, sat on, or used as a medium for clobbering smaller kids and still not lose their identity. Ground goober is sticky enough not to dry out the bread and firm enough not to make it squishy.

And, unlike slicing tomatoes or separating clumps of sprouts, spreading peanut butter is a user-friendly program requiring little dexterity or skill, easy enough for a first grader or his arthritic grandma.

"So what was your favorite school lunch?" Bob had to ask.

"I took a carton of cottage cheese, poured out the cottage cheese, and filled it up with Spaghetti-O's. Did you know you can eat Spaghetti-O's with a sharpened pencil?"

Tot-Spreadable Peanut Butter

Beat and blend a fresh banana or fresh or canned peaches, pears, or applesauce with peanut butter.

Advantages: Less fat than straight PB; fruit provides nutritional boost; economical; softer than PB — no more destroyed bread.

Food Time: I want to do it myself . . .

When tots clamor to serve themselves, it isn't always the food they want, it's the action — shaking out, dipping in, spreading on. Too much action, usually: too much salt, sugar, and fat.

If the objectionable elements of I Want To Do It Myself food can be reduced and the nutritional value increased, then children's urge to shake and spread need not be stifled.

Healthier Spread for Bread

Beat the white of 1 medium egg until stiff and dry. Add this to 1/3 cup margarine and beat until well blended. While beating the mixture, gradually add 2 tablespoons dry powdered milk solids; this serves as a binder. Mixture will be very pale. (Think twice about food coloring; most biochemical-nutritionist-behaviorists are certain it's worse than the fat you're replacing here.) Keep refrigerated. Use in 3 - 4 days.

Advantages: About 1/3 the fat of margarine; contains protein (egg white is nearly 100% protein); soft mixture is bread-friendly, easy to spread.

Sugar-Less Jam

Dissolve 1 rounded teaspoon of sugar-free gelatine in 2/3 cup boiling water. Chill until soft set.

Stir until broken up, but do not beat. Add 1/2 cup of jam; stir to blend. Refrigerate in covered container.

Advantages: Less than half the sugar of jam; less than half the price per serving; thinner mixture is more spreadable and provides portion control — kids can't pile it on.

Tot friendly salt

While nutritionists recommend we not add salt to youngsters' foods, we have to be realistic. Meal time is family time. If Dad salts, children will. (Men use more salt than women do!) Kids don't actually want the salt, they want to shake. Give them something to shake besides sodium.

For the base ingredient, use "light" salt or sodium-free salt substitute. Add flavor-and-fillers: Paprika; onion powder; dry Parmisan cheese; finely powdered dry milk solids; very fine dry parsley flakes. (Butter-flavored sprinkles make superb flavor boosters, but they are costly for kid tables!)

For portion control, use a shaker with very small holes; or tape over all but one or two holes in the cap of an empty seasoning shaker. (Remember, it's the *action* that tots like!) Added incentive: Affix a label with the child's name to his very own, personal, private salt shaker.

27

Learning and language

"That little boy is *smart!* Just listen to him *talk!"*

"Our test scores indicate the child is retarded. Her language skills are extremely undeveloped for her age."

"Listen, if you want to snow Professor Johnson, take two blue books to the history test and fill 'em up. Just write lots and he'll figure you know the stuff. Profs don't have time to read everything, anyway."

SPOTTED OWL, Idaho (Westnews Service) — Students at Spotted Owl Middle School outscored their agemates in the 11 Western States in the National Bird Achievement Test. The N-BAT measures academic progress in nine categories of language and reading and one section of math."

"People judge you by the words you use. If your vocabulary is limited, your opportunities are limited. Order this vocabulary program for ten monthly payments of only . . . ."

It's all true. We are a verbal society. People do judge us, and children are pegged and labeled according to their ability to communicate. Since humans devised languages, language has been *the* yardstick by which we judge a person's brilliance, whether it's an accurate measuring stick or not.

Language is required to process information and formulate ideas and understandings. Linguists say that in order to process information, humans must know the names for the objects being processed. Words first, then concepts; the concrete, then the abstract. Children who do not know the words can not understand the "things."

Have you had the pleasure of watching *Fantasia* with a 2, 3, or 4 year old? Much of its visual stimuli is abstract — squiggles of color, bursts of brightness, patterns and designs without name. The small child is puzzled, even a bit frustrated that the "things" have no name. He doesn't know where to categorize the images, has no directory for processing them, has no base for discerning what to *do* with them.

A teacher who worked in a locale where language and culture were in transition explained it to me this way. "The kids speak pidgin Native and pidgin English. They don't know either tongue well enough to have a language to think in."

Cognizance and communication can be achieved in any language. The important thing is acquiring competence and fluency in *some* language — Old World, New World, throat clicks, or signing.

Humans of all cultures and tongues learn oral language the same way: automatically. They hear, they mimic, process, and repeat. Without formality, children learn the words, the structure, syntax, plurals, pronouns, prepositions, verb forms, grammar, rhythm, inflection, and pitch. Parents, siblings, radio, TV, all the speaking world — they provide stimulus and patterns; but they do not *teach* children to talk.

Language begins before birth. It is now known that unborn babies hear the world outside the womb. It is also generally agreed that the newborn recognizes his mother's voice and from the moment of birth distinguishes hers from all others.

A mother of six told me, "We don't talk to our babies. They can't understand. When kids start to talk, we talk to them." Her kids did not do well in school. They didn't do very well around town, either.

Adeptness with language is the most crucial criteria for academic success in school. Academic skills are based on listening, speaking, reading, and writing. Even math depends on reading the words and understanding them. Most sections of most IQ tests rely on articulating words, meanings, and ideas; thus, the best communicators are labeled the "smartest" people.

There was a time when some psychological-educational theorists said it this way: Language is an intensely personal thing. To mess with a child's use of language is to humiliate him, and to invalidate his home. Don't mess with a child's language.

A lot of us didn't buy the theory. For people of all ages, most oral language occurs in informal, spontaneous, unstructured settings. Adults and peers usually accept a child's words and expressions if he manages to communicate the essence of what he means. But parents and teachers need to *guide* kids. It's incumbent on the adults in charge to assure the *development* of language, as opposed to simply letting kids rattle. Adults need to provide a context for language, to deliberately plan things to talk *about,* and to guide the child in the acquisition of the vocabulary and structure to do so.

HELPING THEM LEARN LANGUAGE

❑ Starting on the baby's day of birth, talk to your child.

❑ Read to your children, long before they can understand the stories.

❑ Teach them the real names of things. There are cars, vans, station wagons, taxis, pick-ups, campers, busses, minibusses, travel homes, and trucks. Dahlias, daffodils, dandelions. Geese, robins, hawks . . . you get the idea. Kids have a greater capacity to differentiate than we think; if they can identify all those characters on Sesame Street, they can distinguish mittens from gloves and an apricot from a peach.

Study after study, decade after decade, yielded the same conclusion: The best readers are kids who were read aloud to, clear through the primary grades. This is the one single ingredient common to good readers, and it applies to all kids, regardless of their cultural, economic, or social standing, or of parents' age, education, occupation, or marital status.

However, future studies might come up with a new result. The highest achieving students beyond the 1990s will prove to be those who were born to healthy, drug-free mothers, and who were adequately nourished in infancy and early childhood.

❑ Encourage kids of all ages to describe, explain, and articulate. What do you do with a hammer? Why do we eat? Explain the steps in making a sandwich. Tell me what the Billy Goats Gruff did. If we went to Philadelphia what would we see? If a stranger offers you a dollar what should you do? What's the difference between Reeboks and L.A. Gears? Why should you have a later curfew, and what time should it be, and what would you do in those four extra hours?

❑ Encourage kids to interpret what they see. Not to simply name things, but to speculate what happened, what will happen, why and how. To intellectualize. Utilize pictures, the weather, people passing by; while you're going places, doing things, or working around the house.

❑ Present opportunities for youngsters to narrate, to tell their own stories. Encourage children of all ages to develop their skills in relating factual, no-fluff knowledge-based information as well as the whole realm of imagination, fantasy, and make-believe.

❑ Turn off the TV.

LANGUAGE LAUNCHERS
  ❑ *PICTURES*

At level 1, infants identify objects. First, he can point to objects you name: Where is the tree; show me the house. At the next step, he will be able to name items and point them out: Kitty; car. Very young children cannot visually distinguish single items from an array; begin with pictures of single objects and proceed gradually to a complete scene.

The steps are pretty much universal for all kids across all cultures. This is how children will interperet pictures as their verbal skills advance:

— Say what the subject (noun) is doing (verb). (Boy play; boy dig.)

— Explain where it is taking place. (Outside; beach; sand.)

— Tell what is being done with objects depicted. (The boy is digging in the sand with the shovel.)

— Predict what will happen next. (He'll put the sand in the bucket.)

— Enumerate the correct sequence of events. (The boy took his shovel and bucket to the beach, dug some sand, put it in the bucket, and poured sand on his daddy.)

— Conjecture various things that may happen afterward. (Make a sand castle; pour sand on the daddy.)

— Make up a story about the picture. The length, depth, and creativity of the story depend upon the child's exposure and experience to story-telling, his degree of imagination, his lack of inhibition, and his level of verbal competence.

— Relate realistically the cause, effect, and relationship of events and phenomena. The degree of accuracy regarding why things happen is based upon the child's base of knowledge.

— Suggest options or alternatives to what is being depicted. (The dog might catch the cat; or the cat might hiss and scratch and chase the dog off; or the animals might be friends and the dog is just making noise because dogs are supposed to.)

Children deal with real objects and events first. Imagination comes later.

❑ VIDEOS AND TV

What's "right" for youngsters depends upon the tastes and preferences of the adult in charge, and the goals the adult has for the child. "Good" kiddie programs develop intellectual and verbal skills. They foster interaction. That is, they draw out little viewers to sing along; they provide repetetive segments for children to join in ("Who's tripping over my bridge?").

Good programs have less blabber and fewer ka-pow sound effects and more silent spaces where viewers can *think*. Electronic wonders do not foster language development if the electronic wonders do not allow viewers to get a word in over the noise.

Two excellent videos which literally *make* children narrate a story as they watch: *Milo and Otis* and *The Snowman*.

❑ TOYS

You can't keep children from talking as they play; most kids keep up a running commentary. The toys the adult provides will determine the *kind* of commentary kids keep running. If adults wish their children to learn to communicate with hostility and revenge, they will carefully provide toys of war and interracial hatred.

Good talkstarter toys: Families of dolls and animals. Select dolls that don't DO anything. Put the child in control, not the doll.

Items for playing house.

Tools, pretend ones or real. Girls are into Home Improvement, too, erruuh, erruuh.

Boxes and cartons, all sizes and shapes.

Dress-up clothes, hats, shoes, purses, jewelry. Second-handers.

Spoons, shovels, containers; mud, sand.

Blocks, trucks, wagons; items of construction.

Appropriate toys enhance every facet of kids' development. Balance verbal and intellectual activities with equipment for the physical person. Youngsters benefit from equipment they can pull, push, peddle, paddle, climb, throw, catch, lift, balance on, jump from, and dance to. They even benefit from — I can scarcely believe I'm going to say this — skateboards.

> The most important ingredients for academic success are nutrition, language, and self-esteem.

28

Overloading the circuits

Driving past the grade school building at dusk, the two mothers had a clear view inside the brightly lit classrooms. Custodians at work, undoubtedly; the teachers' parking lot was almost empty. The five rooms facing the street looked very much alike. Children's art projects and papers covered the walls, the windows, even dripped from the ceiling, mobile-fashion. They were marked, probably, "Good work!" . . . "Neat writing"; or with Star, Smilie, Care Bear, or Kermit stickers.

The mothers stopped before the schoolhouse and studied.

"There's too much stuff. It's . . . *nervous*," one mother said.

"It's cluttered. It's supposed to be inspiring. Attractive. And give the kids positive strokes — Your Work Is Good Enough To Be Posted," said the second.

"If they spend the schoolday in a room like this, how can I convince my girls *their* rooms should be barren and tidy?"

"The kids in those rooms are getting an overload. There is so much stuff it overwhelms them. When they don't know where to focus, they shut down all systems and don't concentrate on any of it." The second mom has held teaching certificates in two states but quit teaching because "it's too political."

The vast majority of elementary classrooms look very much like these, and they are counterproductive. Living in a mess is exactly the wrong approach to learning.

Hyperactivity is a disturbance of the neurological circuits and the body's chemical plant. The hyperactive is unable to focus, concentrate, and be attentive. (Hyperactivity is not an emotional disorder and it is not rooted in flawed rearing, as was so long believed. A hyper child is *not* the mother's fault.)

The figures vary according to the research and the researcher, but it's generally agreed that from 3 to 10 percent of American kids and 5 percent of Canadians suffer Attention Deficit Hyperactivity Disorder (ADHD). Some experts believe that as many as 20 percent of school agers have ADHD, says Dr. John F. Taylor in his book *Helping Your Hyperactive Child* (Prima Publishing, 1990. If you wonder if you have a hyper, *get the book!*). Add to those the number of kids having Attention Deficit Disorder but who are not hyperactive; plus the 7 percent of school kids with learning disabilities . . . .

What stimulates a malfunctioning system to wiggles, wildness, and tantrums? What stimulus cases the system to shut down, to withdraw to a place inside itself where it's quiet, and not pay attention to the things around it? What stimulates kids is *too much* stimulus. Too many colors, too-bright lights, too much stuff. Some of the problems in the schoolroom are brought on *by* the schoolroom. Plenty of studies verify that.

So why would teachers go around shooting themselves in the foot?

Reason One. Administrators like "stimulating, attractive classrooms." (Until recent years, very few principals had actually taught in the primary grades, so whatever they favor isn't always based upon experience.) In one of my districts, an education specialist's job was to go around evaluating teachers, to rate them and grade them on their teaching ability and effectiveness.

"I don't have time to sit in classrooms and watch everyone teach," he once told us. "But I can tell by the Motivational Bulletin Boards (he always said it in capital letters, sacred-like) who the good ones are." He had a favorite saying: "She's one of the best damn teachers in this state. She has the best damn Motivational Bulletin Boards you ever saw." He said this of just about everyone, and we always wondered who was *not* one of the best damns.

Two. Visitors and viewers believe that having a lot of stuff hanging around means the kids have been busy. Good PR for the school and the individual teachers.

Three. Posting a child's work delivers public applause, those positive strokes that kids so urgently need. It does wonders for a youngster to know his work is good enough to tape on the wall. (The same reason you magnet his stuff to the refrigerator at home.)

Four. Teachers compete. It's a contest to have the "most stimulating, most attractive room." Clutter equals quality. Item Four is the result of items one, two, and three. I can tell you the competition is serious: teachers who aren't art minors spend hundreds of dollars on room decorations and bulletin board fixings.

General rule: The lower the age, the higher the overload. High school teachers aren't very big on room decorations. Elementary and secondary people have different approaches: Grade school teachers say, "I teach *kids*." High school teachers say "I teach *chemistry*." (This subtle difference is a credit to elementary teachers.)

Does all this mean I think teachers ought to take the stuff down?

Yes.

Not to the point of stark, empty, and depressing. But toned down, way down. Selective.

Those tiny cubicles special ed kids get relegated to may not be as learning-negative as you think. An undecorated, uncluttered, undistracting vacated broom closet or storage room is a better setting in which to tutor remedial students than a blazing, blaring classroom.

And while you're rearranging the schoolroom to induce attention, orderliness, and learning, trade in the blue fluorescents for soft white-to-moonglow. A years-ago study of the physical qualities of various ballasts indicated that blue fluorescents stimulate human electrical circuitry into overfiring. They trigger nervousness, restlessness, and disorderliness, and aggravate both hyperactivity and epilepsy.

All the above applies to the home environment as well.

I concluded that kids don't pay much attention to the stuff on the bulletin boards, anyway. To test it out, I once posted the questions and answers to Friday's State History exam. Nobody noticed; nobody aced the test.

One term I saw all except seven of the students in our high school every day, most of them in at least two classes. One week I posted a notice on my bulletin board, typed on construction paper of an attention-grabbing, clangy shade of orange.

TEN FREE POINTS
IN THE CLASS OF YOUR CHOICE
TELL ME YOU SAW THIS NOTICE AND CLAIM
YOUR POINTS WHEREVER YOU ARE NEEDY
No catches. No gimmicks
Sorry...offer applies only to my classes. SH

In the entire school, only one student claimed his
points.

What over stimulates is . . . too much stimulation.
When a child is overloaded, he shuts down. If you
want him to learn to focus, to remain calm and
attentive, subdue and simplify. Weed out the clutter.

29

They don't teach like they used to

Wannabe writers often send me manuscripts "to look at." Bombeckian columns, some of them; or science fiction shorties, heavy-reading self-help pop-psychs, or full-length novels seeking hardback covers. Most of the authors apologize for their lack of literary polish, then defiantly add, "But I never took any formal writing classes and didn't do well in school grammar." They are like musicians trying out for the symphony without knowing any key signatures.

One of the Great American Hopefuls sent such a piece — it's hard to acclaim as serious a novel that is written as a single paragraph — and he passed the buck for his technical shortfalling. "My teachers should have made me work harder." His next comment: "The education system was better in the Forties, when I was in school. They don't teach like they used to."

"No, they don't," I said, but I didn't bother to elaborate.

My grade school had none of those "reading groups" intended to provide each youngster appropriate challenge and success. All the kids in my third grade . . . fourth . . . fifth . . . read the same dippy stories from the same book at the same time, even if they couldn't read them — and even if they had surpassed that level years ago. In the fourth grade, three of us girls kept Earl Stanley Gardeners from the town library in our desks, to "read in your spare time, so you won't talk." We also took our turns standing to read aloud from *Friendly Village* .

Some kids couldn't read *Friendly Village* very well, but that was no excuse for destroying them. I was horrified at my teacher's awful insensitivity the day she called Eddie down. She adjusted her face into weariness and pain. "Eddie," she said slowly and mournfully, "it's just torture listening to you read.

But I guess I can't skip you every time. Stand up. The rest of you," she addressed the stunned class, "take a nap."

We took those My Weekly Reader tests every month or six weeks, and the teacher posted the list on the bulletin board for all the world to see: who scored what, with a red line drawn across the page. That was the grade-level mark. Names below the line were the ones who flunked the test, and the teaching strategy was to give them hell in front of everyone. Positions above and below the red line never changed, so her form of hell never did anything except to keep the failures in a constant state of it.

When we memorized maps in the sixth grade, we filled in Prussia and French West Africa and the Byzantine Empire on the outline maps, a different color for each country; you needed the big box of crayons. Some of the states of 1938 Europe were extinct by the time I was in sixth grade, but the school had old books and that's what the old books said and the books were gospels and the teacher never said the world had turned. Seven years later my sister used the same maps and learned the same errors. The new Brasilia wasn't on the old maps, and we still had to learn to spell Constantinople.

History was one subject and Geography another, and the geography book didn't mention Napoleon because Napoleon is history and History is a different subject. Spelling and Language were separate subjects, so the teacher didn't checkmark a misspelled word in your Language story nor non-agreement of subject and verb in your Spelling sentences. You needed to spell correctly only when your paper was headed Spelling. Male high school teachers bragged they couldn't spell, and that classed Spelling as a sissy subject.

When I was a senior we got to Teapot Dome in American History. To me Teapot Dome was the death blow to the "Our Wondrous American Heritage" theory. First the Spaniards were so appalled at the Aztecs' savagery that the conquistadores savagely annihilated the culture. Then we discover Washington and Jefferson had slaves but it was okay because . . . well, because they were Washington and Jefferson, and they were *nice* to *their* slaves. Then the Indian Problem and Manifest

Destiny and the carpetbaggers and the muckrakers and yellow journalism and the spoils system, then the Japanese "encampments" and now, Teapot Dome.

I raised my hand, got called on, and said, "America is supposed to have such a glorious history and we are supposed to be so proud of what we were and are. I don't see much to be proud of."

The teacher scowled very hard, then in his boomy basso he said, "Well, Susan, if you don't see it I feel sorry for you."

What I thought then was, *He doesn't see it, either. He's a coach who has to teach something, so they gave him a textbook he could read aloud to us.* What I thought later, when I learned things that weren't in the textbook, was that maybe the coach was afraid the McCarthyites had bugged the classroom.

The correct way to get information in 1952 was to go to the library and look it up, even though our little school library didn't have the things you were supposed to look it up in. If you memorized the *list* of things to look up things in, you got a good grade in first quarter sophomore English. That way, if you ever got to some place like Seattle, you'd know what library book to look in to find the answers . . . if you happened to get to the library while you were in Seattle. In 1952, the only correct answers were what the World Book said, even though our World Books were printed in 1938.

Around 1951 the grade school had a big housecleaning. They threw away all the 1938 textbooks. Everyone was horrified — students, teachers, taxpayers. Why would the school toss out all those perfectly good books, so filled up with Truth.

A lot of teachers and people were convinced most of the Class of 53 was headed straight to Skid Row because they were so *bad*. A half dozen of them smoked cigarettes and two of the guys skipped school once. On the plus side, every single kid in the class held some kind of job while they were in high school. Back in those antique days, teachers and people approved of working students. And: there was a correlation — Kids who worked the longest hours got the best grades, unless they were going steady. The Great American Novelist is right. They don't teach like they used to.

30

What happened to our parents?

By RYAN JOHN SPICKARD

Ryan John Spickard attends Cleveland High School, Seattle, Washington. In addition to writing, he seriously pursues drawing, skiing, and music both classical and rock. In this article, Ryan drops the shortfallings of youth on the feet of their parents.

What happened to you all? Why did you stop trying to make us understand the need for justice, for teaching us the way to better the world?

Yes, you! The parents. This is addressed to you, because you forgot to teach us so much.

I can remember when we had to strain our necks to look up at the giants who kept us warm and safe. Those giants that could ease away our uncertainties with a calm word and a soft song. Those giants that looked down upon us with an expression that told us as long as they were there, no harm would fall into our fragile world.

Those days seem to have disappeared right along with our role models. Then, whatever we witnessed we thought must be right; why would you show us how to do wrong? Now we know better. We have grown to the point where we can make decisions on our own and understand the consequences of our actions. Most of those actions we can deal with; and the others, well, we can at least live with.

You taught us to walk, to talk, to go to the bathroom by ourselves. You taught us to throw a ball, ride a bike, and use a knife and fork. You taught us almost everything except how to be ourselves; from a mother's ambition to make her daughter into a "good little girl," to the father's ambition to make his son into a "MAN," you have poked, prodded, pushed, and shoved us toward what you wanted us to be.

If shoving us off a cliff was the only way you could have us live up to parental standards, then every teenager in the world would be piled on top of each other at the bottom of that cliff. That is a lot of adolescent humans.

What is the most common worry of the parents of suburbia? Their children's grades in high school. Granted, that is a valid concern — we do understand that knowledge is power; but there are more pressing problems to pay attention to: the social part of an education. This is the most confusing and frightening time we will have in our lives. Our grades add just another stress for the teenage body to deal with. Stress you dumped on.

"Report card time" is looked upon with dread. If parents encouraged good grades instead of demanding them, we would view poor grades with disappointment in failing ourselves instead of you.

We are not addressing you to point a finger and damn you for screwing up our lives, but as a plea. To ask you to find out what we aspire to, what we dream of, and what we really need in our lives.

In our adolescence there comes a point when our innocence becomes crooked, sometimes savagely crooked; and it is then that the millions of questions — not hundreds of thousands, but millions — need to be answered. Most of these we are going to find out about on our own, like it or not. But those that are left we still need help on. *We still need your help.*

31

Non achievers, non achievement

Shelli was a luminous light in the small high school where I taught. Teachers and townspeople alike knew she was destined to become a positive contributor in the near future. She could do everything, and do it better than almost everyone. But only if it required no effort.

She cursed aloud when homework was assigned — then didn't do it. "Give me class time," she demanded. But then, so did all the kids. In our school, and in high schools throughout our district, teachers, though they disapproved, had to live by the rule the students had imposed in Year One: We work on class time or we don't work.

"Maybe Shelli is unchallenged; bored," we said. We created a Gifted and Talented program in the high school and put her in the high-flying track. She never completed her first project; she chose to return to her comfortable level of boredom.

Everyone in town was greatly pleased when Shelli went off to college, and equally surprised when, shortly after the start of her second semester, she returned. She was the first one to admit she couldn't cut it.

"I blame the education system and all my teachers from first grade on," she wrote me after she returned home. "They didn't challenge me. They didn't make me work."

A few years earlier, in another school in another town, Murray, another bright student who wasted his potential equally well, wrote an essay. "If students refuse to work, it's the teacher's fault. The teacher is the hit man."

After announcing the results of Oregon students' 1991 achievement tests, State School Superintendent Norma Paulus analyzed the results: academic learning largely shuts down after eighth grade. That analysis comes as no surprise to anyone who works with teenagers.

But there's a fallacy in the Establishment's conclusion

that this non-achievement is wholly and solely the fault of the schools and the people who staff them. That conclusion decrees that by age 14, 16, 18, *H. sapiens teenagerus* is incapable of inner drive, ambition, self-determination; of responsibility for its own actions, its own destiny.

Teachers from diverse points in many states tell me that high school kids do, in fact, decide, prioritize, set goals. They decide their highest priority is their part-time job, because their goal is to own and maintain a Driving Machine and the Sound System that goes in it, and the disks and tapes to put in that.

"Very quickly, the 17-year-old worker is 'promoted' to assistant night manager at the pizza place," explains an Anchorage teacher. "The student figures it's easy to work up to the top and that he's qualified to be there. So who needs history, anyway? For kids with part-time jobs, school itself is soon history."

But then, this is real-life experience, and the students are learning the work ethic.

And what a work ethic it is. The ethic where carpenters won't carry sheetrock, electricians won't sweep up their own rubble, repairmen won't guarantee their work for more than 30 days. The ethic of featherbedding, goldbricking, doing your nails on company time, and It Isn't What You Know, It's Who. Of buyer beware and never buy anything made on Monday.

Learning does not, either, shut down after eighth grade. High school kids learn all the above, and they also learn that they can not be fired for incompetence, no matter how incompetent. If one is fired, one can always allege it is because of some prejudice of person, place, or persuasion. If a student flunks, he learns that the same forces are responsible for that, too, and he can grieve it and win.

So we keep tossing more lambs on the altar, tying more whipping boys to the pillar. That highschoolers skid downward is made to be the fault of the school system, the curriculum, administrators, teachers, legislators, the State Superintendent; of parents, preachers, and Madonna. Blame the kids' shortfalling on lack of funding. Blame the test scores on the test itself; on racism, sexism, politics, sociology, latchkeys, psychology, demographics, economics. Blame it on the Congress and the Presidency, who squabble over everything as if *they* were school kids.

Every high school has its Shellis, its Murrays, its night managers. They devote their studenthood to passing blame, and it becomes the thing they do best . . . and it works. So far, the kids themselves have been held faultless. Nobody has yet suggested that underachievement might be the responsibility of the underachievers.

> It's The System's responsibility to provide the opportunities. It's the youngster's responsibility to seize them.

4

The Emerging Person

Branches and buds

32

Long way, babies

When does a tentative idea turn into an accepted concept? When does something that's merely being tried out become an established practice? Most of what we call changes, especially social and educational ones, come not as eruptions but as evolutions. Perhaps they assumed form in another epoch, unperceived, like a star that is born a million years before we see its light.

In my sophomore year the journalism teacher appointed me editor. Our monthly newspaper (which my mother named when she attended that school in 1929) was universally acknowledged as the best school paper in the county — and now . . . it . . . was . . . *Mine!*

It had long irked me that the only stars in our school were the athletes, and no one else got any recognition. I mentioned it to my dad. He agreed, much to my surprise — in the 1920s my dad was a football hero at Benson Tech in Portland and he even, I think, won a letter at Oregon State.

"But that's the way it is," he said, "and always will be." He raised his bushy brows, the familiar warning sign. "So don't you be the one to go stirring things up."

When I was a junior, still editing, I decided to try my hand at stirring things up anyway. Power-crazed, I guess. I wrote an editorial: "Are Athletics Overemphasized in Our School?" A rhetorical question, of course, for, exercising the Persuasive Writing skills I learned in English Two, I persuasively proved the answer was Yes. Seizing the penned podium, I praised, perhaps for the first time in the history of our school, the accomplishments and abilities of other students — mostly musicians, since I was a klutz on the court but a blast in the band.

It was bold. It was risky. Before I even turned the piece in, I could already feel the tentacles of ostracization curling around me. I'm soon to be on the outs with all the boys, my right brain said. *What the hell, you were never in,* said my left. *What you ought to worry about is that you haven't taken American History yet, because that's the coach's class.* I also expected the irony would not escape the English Two teacher, to whom I owed so much of my skills as a penman: she was the head coach's wife.

I doubted my editorial would ever play. So doubtful that I attached a P.S. to the journalism teacher: "If this isn't printed, I will resign." Then I typed copies for all the other teachers, in case they'd never see it in print.

I had never been a skiff-rocker, so I have no idea why I did this, except I believed that education should be about the qualities of mind, talent, and hard work more than about busting the bones of some poor "enemy" from Valley High School.

You have to understand something. This was 1951, when there was no such word as *protest* and nobody had heard of Berkeley, and when there was no such concept as student control of *anything* and high school kids were only expected to memorize, not analyze . . . when girls' equal-anything was uninvented and sports for boys was *the* activity.

I didn't resign. I was fired.

But . . . That year the school began giving service pins to students in every academic activity and extra-curricular organization, and letters — *Letters!* — to all bandsmen.

My sister Jane followed me through school, seven years later. Now it's 1959, and she wants to take physics.

"Girls don't need physics," growled the teacher. "Never had any girls in physics, never will."

Jane *had* heard the word protest, and she did. The superintendent, however, supported his teacher. So my sister mentioned it to Dad, and this time he was ready to *help* his kid stir things up.

"Okay," the teacher told my sister, still growling. "But you have to recruit another girl so you'll have a lab partner. I'm not going to have mixed partnerships in my lab, just in case you're here looking for dates."

There were three straight-A physics students that year. Two of them were girls.

"So I was seventeen when I figured out that any woman who has the grit can compete in a man's domain," my sister told me thirty years later. "But it wasn't that I wanted to do better than any guys. I wanted to do better than *anyone*."

"Yeah," I agreed. "When you're in physics or when you play trombone, you can't afford to do it only medium-good."

The human race emerged in many places, all about the same epoch. Your home may very well be the stirring-place of its own Mesopotamia, or Valley of the Nile, or its own Ganges or Hwang Ho Valley. Your very own children may be trying out the new ideas that will become the social changes of their time. Let them stir.

33

S O A R !

"I spend a quarter of my teaching time, one way or another, building kids up," I said. "Their lack of self-esteem gets in the way of everything they try to do."

"I spend more time than that," said Dan, grade school computers and high school PE. "Trying to convince them they're okay transcends everything else I do, in class and out. Kids who don't think well of themselves have insurmountable learning blocks."

"They have more blocks than that." Eric, the 8th grade teacher, put on the third pot of coffee that wintry Saturday at his house. "Tell me who's drifting, who's hostile, who's in trouble around town. Tell me the social problems, the abusers, the self-destructive . . . and I'll go right down the line and match them, name for name, with the kids who think they're no good."

"It's not just kids," said Barbara, grade 2. "Kids without self-esteem become adults with no anchor. If they don't think well of themselves by the time they go out our door, they never will."

"Society's entire approach is stated in the negative," said Val, 3rd grade. Together, the five of us represented 77 years of teaching, in case experience equals wisdom. "It's all Just Say No. What are kids supposed to say Yes to?"

"To themselves," Eric said. "But too many of them have no idea how to do that. I gave my kids a little self-assessment quizzeroo, and they could not identify even two or three things they can do well. Not even the kids who have formidable talents."

"It's not cool to talk yourself up," Val said, nodding.

"It's more serious than that," Dan said. "Too many kids simply seem to *accept* that they don't amount to anything. Inside every child there's a competent person trying to emerge, but too many kids give up on themselves before the person has a chance to form."

119

The sense of self-worth is a product a long time in the making. In the most confident, competent persons it has been nurtured since birth, since the newborn's bare skin touched his mother's, since someone held and stroked and talked to him and applauded his first step, his first scribble, his first song, and when he learned to throw and jump and pump himself in a swing and hit a teeball, and when he learned to write his name and play a clarinet and parallel park and fill out his application for college.

If the sense of self-worth has long been dormant, it is possible to cultivate it and bring it to bloom when kids are older, though its roots will never grow as deep nor its stem as strong.

The basic strategies for guiding the development of self-esteem are remarkably similar for everyone, whatever their age. I can reduce it to a simple formula:

SELF-ESTEEM = Opportunity, Appreciation, Recognition. SOAR.

OPPORTUNITY

Okay, it's checklist time. Which of these can YOU do well:

___ Shape a horse shoe

___ Make papyrus from a cattail

___ Shinny up a coconut tree

___ Skin and cure a mastadon hide

___ Extract and process flour from manioc

___ Keep a coal alive, kindle a buffalo chip fire

___ Communicate in Aramaic

By now you've caught on: These skills are of another time and place, of different tools and technologies. You don't do them because yours is not the lifetime to get the chance to learn them.

Okay, then, for things that are today and real, Checklist Two. For which of these do you have ability:

❑ Play the Irish pennywhistle

❑ Scrimshaw on irory

❑ Propogate a new species of dahlia

- ❏ Disassemble and repair a bassoon
- ❏ Animate, film, edit a cartoon
- ❏ Translate Inyupiaq to Papuan
- ❏ Compute the American dollar value of rupees invested at 11.43% compounded biquarterly held for 16 months 12 days and converted to Krugerrands

The correct answer is you don't know whether you possess these capabilities unless you have had the chance to try the task. You don't even know what things are out there to be tried unless those things are presented to you, one way or another. It's up to the adults in charge to present those opportunities to children.

The quickest way to make a child feel good about himself is for him to be able to *do* things — whatever those things are, whatever his level of intellect, development, and accomplishment.

Parents must provide things for kids to do things *with.* Reubens and Michaelangelo and Picasso could not have developed their talent if they had never had a paintbrush in their hands. Your little artist will not start on his way until you give him his first crayons, preferably when he is so young he doesn't yet know he isn't supposed to eat them.

By and large, schools do a better job of providing exposure and exploration than individual homes. For a couple of reasons.

First, kids who haven't discovered any of their talents feel inferior. Dumb. Kids who think they're dumb fulfill the prophecy, usually before you realize what's happening. They fall behind in school and they become bored. Disruptive. Teachers employ heroic measures to tap children's resources, to identify aptitudes that may lead the child to fields of interest. With the bored, the spacey, the disruptive . . . well, frankly, teachers' heroic measures sometimes have something to do with self-defense.

Second, schools have on hand a wealth of materials to expose kids to opportunities, more things than a household could possibly afford. Dozens of artistic mediums, scores of musical instruments and activities, scads of athletic supplies and physical equipment. And the people who know how to use them. Folks who call these things frills are foolish.

APPROVAL

You stayed awake nights creating your project and you worked overtime to perfect it, and you know it is the best one anyone in your company ever turned in. The boss never said Good Job, never thanked you ... never even mentioned it. How does it feel?

Did you ever ignore a child's Good Job?

Many would argue that the correct word should be Affection, not Approval. In case semantics are that important, I argue that we love the *child*, and we approve of his *accomplishments*. Praise, applause, cheers, and approval are crucial, whether it's a two-month-old's first smile or a college-bounder's scholarship from the Kiwanis Club. But you do not expect the Kiwanians to *fall in love* with your child of achievement any more than you expect your boss to fall in love with you for a job well done.

There is something, however, that adults need to understand and they need to get right. Praise and approval must be honest and sincere. The child has to earn it, and the adult has to mean it. Otherwise it's phony and contrived, and everyone knows it. If a fourth grader finally spells *cat* and *dog*, it isn't a cause for public proclamation. When a 13-year-old cleans his room, or gets his homework done and turned in, it isn't something to make a big deal over, because that's what he's supposed to do. You don't get a merit raise for working a full shift; that's the minimum; it's expected.

Nor does approval mean the absence of disapproval. If you disapprove of the disaster area he calls his room, say so. Expressing your disapproval, and laying out what you want done instead, is one of a parent's guidance duties. Sometimes that's difficult, because the line between critical guidance and haranguing criticism is a fine one.

RECOGNITION

The quickest and surest way for a youngster to know she is a swell person is for someone to tell her so. When teachers post their students' pretty penmanship, moms display kiddie drawings, and grandmothers fill their walls with snaps, they are according exactly the kind of recognition that builds children's self-esteem, pride, and security. No silly old grandma's bragging ever damaged a child's self-image, especially if the child was in earshot.

The more public the recognition, the greater the benefit, for nothing begets success like success. Kids can find successes in plays and programs, where kiddies are put on stage, to be applauded (the best chance to get to be in a program is at church); in team and individual sports, music recitals, spelling bees. In Campfire, Scouts, 4-H, a supermarket color-the-jack-o'-lantern contest (they display all the entries, you know). Marching in a community parade; being the leader of Follow the Leader or The One To Pass The Sandwiches at a family picnic. All these are recognitions and some do not require competition. All build self-confidence and a sense of belonging.

Unfortunately, the idea of self-esteem, and the theory behind it, has been maligned and mishandled and bent out of shape, like so many other ideas that started out as good ones and got institutionalized into monstrosities. Convincing people they're not much good, then convincing them they need a product to cure it, is big business. Cover titles like "Why The Inner You Is A Maggot" and "Seventeen Ways To Feel Good About Yourself" sell magazines, and slogans telling you that *after all, you're worth it* sell products. There are big bucks in the feel-good business as self-shingled experts and opportunists sell seminars, counseling, books, warm-fuzzy holdies, and stars, stamps, and stickers.

Criticism of the "feel-good movement" is justified. Praise and approval have been misused. To ensure children of successes, we tell them the answers, we solve their problems for them; then we say, "Good job!" When little Ermatrude throws a hissie and smashes the china, we tell her gently, "Honey, you are a terrific person and I adore you but . . . . " Instead of teaching, guiding, and disciplining, we convey the notion that success means someone else's predetermined "right answer," and the delusion that no matter what they do, they're terrific people.

And "lack of self-esteem" has become a Nationally Recognized Excuse. He got snockered and heisted the bank because he has a low opinion of himself. The car's design is flawed because the engineer lacks a sense of self worth. The mechanic didn't replace the O-ring because he doesn't feel good about himself.

Nevertheless, misusing and misguiding the concept of self worth does not make it valueless. Self-confidence is a real thing, and its absence devastates. Any critics who believe self-esteem is baloney, I invite them to visit my high school kids.

HOW TO NURTURE SELF-ESTEEM

❑ Be an interested participant in your kids' activities.

❑ Hold firmly the conviction that *your* kids have talents and potentials inside themselves. Expose them to every possible experience, activity, and opportunity to help them identify and tap their talents, and which will provide their base of knowledge, creativity, socialization, and concepts of the world and their place in it.

❑ When a youngster shows interest in an a concept, an area of knowledge, a creative endeavor, or an idea or activity, capitalize on that interest: encourage the development of information and skills which will lead him to become proficient in that area.

❑ Provide the tools for developing competencies: the things to do things with.

❑ Urge, encourage, and insist if you have to, that your youngsters explore whatever your community offers in cultural, creative, educational, and organizational opportunities.

❑ Never fail to praise, applaud, thank, encourage, bolster, and brag about their talents, skills, and genuine accomplishments. Likewise, do not give them falsely high ratings nor praise undeserved.

❑ Do not expect kids to perform beyond their development and maturity. Reserve undue criticisms. A two- or three-year-old is not a finished product; he is not a miniature adult and he cannot behave and achieve like an older child. (Dads do this the most.)

❑ Talk with youngsters. Give each one-on-one time and attention.

❑ Tell them, straight-out, that they are swell persons.

❑ Give each child chances to do things well, and celebrate it when they do.

❑ Turn off the TV.

34

From conceit to self-worth

Depending on the decade and the school of popular psychology, the terms are Positive self-image, Sense of self-worth, Self-esteem; Affirmative inner motivational style; I'm Worth It; and Ommmm.

It hasn't always been respectable for one to think well of oneself. In the thirties and forties, anyone who did was called Conceited and Conceit was cardinal. What is admired today as Self-Confidence was scorned then as Cocky. So the self-confident kids of my generation had the cockiness beat out of them and my generation made a whole generation of shrinks very rich.

The youth of the late sixties - early seventies refused to be beaten down, and their culture countered with You're OK, I'm OK. Many of the Seventiers interpereted OKism to mean I'm A Perfect Product Just As I Am, No Improvement Required So What Do You Mean I Don't Get An A/ The Job/ Lead Guitar.

After that it was Looking Out For Number One, and that gave everyone dog-eat-dog license, whether it was done ethically or not.

Now we are full circle, backwards. Now one of our urgent priorities is to transform a youngster's deficit of conceit into exuberent self-confidence.

35

A compelling interest

Somewhere between ages six and eight, most youngsters begin to be able to channel their energies to particular areas of interest. Between 6 and 12, the years Dr. Thomas Armstrong of the National Parenting Center calls "the heart of childhood," kids are big on hobbies. They like to collect and categorize things. Some of their pursuits are solitary: Collections and constructions, and emerging skills in physical prowess and individual athletics and in creative endeavors in art, music, or imagination.

Most of the time, though, 6 to 12 are years of perpetual motion and whirling social activity. Heart-of-childhood kids are tireless machines — bikes, skates, jumpropes; sports of all kinds, whether they are skilled and co-ordinated or not. They form exclusive "best pal" friendships; but mostly, they are flockers and joiners. They join clubs or form their own, and they affiliate themselves with special groups of friends.

Now the peer group replaces the parents as the child's prime influence; his driving forces are his social setting and his interests outside the family circle. You'd better hope that by the time your child steps through the school door, the twig is bent.

It's fortunate that kids begin to acquire skills and interests during these years, becuse this is exactly the time they will need them. A compelling interest serves as a coping tool, a survival mechanism a youngster can call up when it is most needed. Let me explain.

On a computer service's "Parenting" bulletin board, members post note after note telling the same story after story. Responses from parents on the network are generally alike, too, ranging from empathy to supportiveness to kick-in-the-pants when it's called for. Here are paraphrases of some representative notes and replies.

My son entered first grade knowing how to read. It's February, and he hasn't read a thing in school yet. They color, cut, and paste, but they don't read. Already, school bores him. What can I do?

"This sounds like my daughter when she started school. Teaching children to add and subtract, read and write before they start school doesn't seem to benefit them any because the school doesn't follow up and maintain their skills, anyway.

"You could try talking with the teacher about your son's capabilities, but they'll probably just tell you, 'That's not what we do in first grade.'

"I encouraged my girl to develop her interests in drawing and writing stories. Then, instead of being bored, she gave herself something constructive and creative to do that she enjoyed."

"Your son needs a library card! Let him take books of his choice to school and read them there. If he can read, he can write about it. Get him a couple of notebooks and some colored felt pens to keep at school.

"Explore things of the world with your boy, find out what grabs his interest, and capitalize on it. Children who develop compelling interests develop the capacity to endure!

"It seems like it's so much easier to change our individual children than it is to change the schools."

"When my son was in first grade, he studied his encyclopedia at school He could identify each European country by its outline and draw every flag from memory. His teacher confiscated his things — "This isn't what we do in first grade." He started school fascinated by science and the world; but his interests were immediately squashed. He pretty much languished until college.

"Now our grown-up kids worry that school won't address their children. My husband and I have decided if the public schools stifle them, we'll scrape up the price of sending our grandkids to private schools."

My son's second grade teacher says he is disruptive and inattentive. I think he spends more time in Time Out than he spends in his seat. He is only a barely average student, but he says school is boring. What can I do?

"A lot of kids that age chatter, act out, and bounce off the walls to get attention. Give your son as much quality time as you can, and while you do, point him in the direction of various things that might catch his interest. If you get him interested in cars or planes, for instance, or in animals or a sport, he could take library books on his topics to school to peruse in his spare time. I did that with my 9-year-old and he began to zero in on his school work so he could finish it and have time for doing what he was interested in.

"It also turned out that my boy isn't average at all. He is quite bright, but not in the areas of the paper work they do at school."

I have seen my fifth grade daughter's homework and I have visited her school and seen what her class is doing. She knew all that stuff two and three years ago. The school has not stimulated or challenged her, and she's bored. Help!

"A bright fifth grader can almost set her own directions! By the time she is 11, a bright child should have developed one or two or more of those vital, driving interests that can so spark kids (and adults, clear through old age). By now she should have the inner motivation to channel her interests. If she does not, light her fire!

"Your girl can use school time profitably and creatively to read, study, write, and organize information about her areas of interest. By that age, the word boredom doesn't have to be in a child's vocabulary, and if it is, it's his or her own making. If she has the ability to work and think independently, she doesn't need to have a teacher or a prescribed curriculum set her agenda."

"My husband is a principal in a school district that operates under teacher tenure, where they can't dismiss incompetents. He says that bright, motivated kids will learn in spite of school."

After my 16-year-old broke up with his girlfriend, he seemed to shut down. He's never had any particular interests in or out of school, so now he has nothing to fall back on. All he does is watch TV, and then he sits and snipes at every story on every show, until his mother and I totally can't stand him. Any suggestions?"

"You identified the problem yourself. He has no interests, so when he hits a snag, he has nothing to fall back on."

"It sounds like your son has been fueled by hormones alone, which, he found out, makes a pretty insecure and imbalanced diet, even for 16. Somewhere in the past ten years, the boy made some choices. Apparently he chose to choose to do nothing, and now, to be nothing. He may or may not now choose to get a life, but you can prod him in that direction. As a counselor, I recommend the following:

"Get your son into the real world. Don't punish him for his world falling apart; but do tell him, firmly and resolutely, that what has collapsed can be reconstructed. At this stage, don't bother to hint or imply what the rules are — flat-out tell him. Put your foot down and don't move.

"Tell him homework is to be done and you'll look at it. He is to be a contributing member of the family — tasks and responsibilities. Make him take in the activities and goings-on at school, basketball games, clean-up day, whatever and anything. Go get a McJob.

"Pull the plug on the TV. Get it out of the house if you have to. Pawn it and use the money to buy reading material that suits a late-teener. Sports Illustrated, Star Trek magazine, Dirt Bike, Gardens & Landscapes, Discovery — anything but TV Guide!

"Keep him too busy to moon around, and while he's about it, he'll probably find some of those compelling interests

130

(that he should have discovered eight or ten years ago!) that will enable him to find the focus, balance, and the skills he needs to ride the waves."

HOW TO HELP YOUR KIDS DEVELOP INTERESTS

❑ Take them to real places of the real world. City, country, outdoors. Botannical gardens and nurseries; petting farm, fish hatchery, aquarium, zoo; concert, art gallery, craft fairs. Fishing, camping, hiking. Ethnic festivals, harvest fairs. Most   are inexpensive or free.

❑ Many communities have free or minimum-fee programs for toddlers through teens. The library, Parks & Recreation, day camps supported by community or fraternals; athletic programs (great or rotten, depending on the coaches and parental pressure to win); Campfire, Scouts, church youth groups; fraternal affiliates (DeMolay, Jobie's, etc.); Boys & Girls Clubs; and so on and on. For high schoolers, volunteer (or even paid) programs such as Candy Stripers, summer parks programs assistants, library aides.

❑ Wherever you go, discuss what you do and see. Relay as much information as you know, even if you think it's over your kids' heads. (We already said they absorb and understand more than we think.)

❑ Expose your kids to music, storytelling and dramatics, arts, crafts, gardening, home care and decorating, needlecraft, cooking, carpentry, mechanicking and fixing things, experimenting in the natural and physical sciences. Guide and instruct in whatever you can, and encourage them to find their own wings in all they can.

❑ Encourage . . . no, insist your kids vicariously explore the world both real and imaginary through books and educational television. Kids should have their own public library cards by the time they are 4 or 5. (And they (! not you!) are responsible for materials they borrow.)

❑   Give kids their own private, personal box for treasures and collections. (Plastic file boxes with lock and carrying handle are perfect for every age.) To encourage recordkeeping and orderliness, supply them with notebooks, scrapbooks and auxiliary materials, and file folders. By junior high, make heroic efforts to have a kid-use typewriter *that works*, even if you must start with a tenth-hand one from a hock shop.

❑   Talk with your kids about what they're doing — take an interest in THEIR interests. And equally important, keep up your own interests and let it be known you're doing so.

36

Teen perspective

BY SONJA ANN MCGUCKEN

Sonja McGucken attends Kingwood High School, Kingwood, Texas. Teenagers are capable of coping with crises, she tells us, if their security is already in place.

In the past, teenagers' big problems were the likes of acne and fitting in the right crowd. Life has changed. The high rate of teen suicides, AIDS, and the terrifying thought of cancer make teen life very complicated.

I remember the clumsy freshmen on the first day of high school, stumbling through the maze of halls, trying to find classes. I did not recognize anyone at all in the halls, until, finally, that one familiar face appeared around the corner. But I adjusted. With the help of the band, I made older friends when I was a freshman.

During high school I found myself in strenuous situations. In my junior year, I received a phone call two hours after school one day, informing me that a classmate and fellow band member had committed suicide. During the same year, three months apart, I lost my aunt and my grandmother to cancer.

From these tragedies I have learned to live my life as it comes and not get upset when things I would like to happen do not. From my ability to cope and adjust, I have lived an easy life compared to other teenagers. My family and friends have helped me to do this, and with their help, I have accomplished much.

37

Play . . . Serious pursuits

Tom Norlin had just played a Shoot The Moon hearts hand.

"You dumb *bleep-bleep!*" Stan (Thorney) Thorne screamed at the man on Tom's left. "It's YOUR *bleep* fault! You should have passed him a *bleep* STOPPER!"

Thorney always played hearts like that. For blood. If he didn't win it was someone's fault. (I played hearts with Thorney twice, eight years between games. The second time was a two-night tournament, and at the end of Night One I was ahead. I didn't show up for the second session; winning seemed too expensive.) "It isn't how you play the game," Thorney once stormed. "It's whether you win."

Lots of people play their games as seriously as Thorney. What we usually overlook is that play is a serious pursuit for children, too. Dr. John Turner, who pioneered the early childhood education program at University of Alaska, Fairbanks, told teachers-in-training: "As the child plays, so the man shall work."

Much of a child's learning comes through play. How he plays can give us insights about his own particular learning styles. From infancy until two years, babies learn about things — what they are, what they can be used for, how they work, and what he can do to gain control of them — by feeling, tasting, dropping, stacking, handling, manipulating.

Katey, 16 months, sat on the sidewalk with a bag of carrots. One by one, she rolled the carrots on the gentle slope in front of her house, intently studying each movement. She pushed them up the hill and down. They did not roll downhill; they rolled in small arcs and circles in front of her. After a while Katey went into the house and brought out a tennis ball and dropped it on the sidewalk and watched it roll down the hill. She brought out a teddy bear, dropped it, then pushed it, and clapped her hands when it went nowhere at all.

Katey couldn't articulate what was happening, but she had obviously grasped a principal of physics: how objects roll depends upon their shape. It was apparent that she learns through observing, experimenting, and confirming. The scientific method. As I watched her, I thought, "If her mother had confiscated those carrots, Katey would have missed a terrific learning experience."

When she was 29 months Katey's parents took her to her first Easter egg hunt. The rule was Parents Stay Out, but parents didn't. By the hundreds, the moms and dads stampeded the lawn at City Park, scooping up eggs and filling their tots' baskets. Katey's folks did not. "We explained it to her," said her dad. "After that, we wanted her to figure it out." Said her mom, "But it sure was hard, Katey being the only child out there on her own."

Katey watched everyone in action. Suddenly her face lit with understanding and she began picking up Easter eggs. Just as her parents intended, she figured it out, then acted. Without help. Observe, confirm. "There's our future CEO," her mom said proudly. She added, "If we'd interfered, she'd have missed a chance to grow."

Around age two, and until about five or six, much of children's play is imaginative. They pretend. When playing together, they announce their parameters: "Pretend like . . . " "Is this grass, or cookies?" Imagining is intellectual, and it is creative. Some of the most fun you'll ever have is eavesdropping on 3, 4, and 5-year-olds' imaginative play.

Between ages 4 and 7, play changes as youngsters develop and mature. They acquire an interest in organized games with rules. They enjoy simple team games like London Bridge and Red Rover. But competitions declaring individual winners isn't a good idea at this age. If a child has a competitive nature, it will emerge; but four to seven is too soon to deliberately introduce ways to designate a child a "loser."

Some of the textbook experts say that at this age boys' and girls' play becomes differentiated; but preschool teachers tell us it happens before four. Girls tend to play more quietly and in a smaller area. They are more apt to take turns and they enjoy rhythms and chants — jump rope and hopscotch and singing games. Little girls' gymnastics are along the lines of cartwheels, somersaults, and balance beams; while boys the same age take to the derring-do of monkeybars and tree-climbing.

Boys are rambunctious, rough and tough. They range over a larger territory than girls and they seem to have a natural instinct for games of conflict.

When I taught kindergarten in rural Alaska, my assistant and I were concerned that the boys turned every opportune item into weapons. We put a moratorium on long blocks, building logs, and rulers. The boys used fingers and sound effects and shot one another, anyway.

Well, after all, the staple foods in this region were from the hunt. Every household held two, four, a half dozen guns. "But they are strictly for subsistence," the aide said. "My people do not use them to hurt other people."

"Must be the movies," I said. Television had not yet arrived in the native villages, but everyone gathered for the weekly movies. The favorites were Bob Hope, war, and John Wayne.

Undoubtedly, we both were wrong. We know now that in almost every culture, every society, boys' play includes conflict and warfare. Some call it hostile, some, protective. Whichever it is, sociologists believe it's instinctive. It isn't taught, and we can't prevent it. However, in our culture some things that are instinctive are nevertheless disallowed in some contexts, including "playing war" in my classroom.

It's hard to know for certain which gender-different activities are inate and which are cultural, but current evidence says more of it may be inborn than learned. The real "us" is deep inside the marrow of the twig; the "culture" part is a veneer. "Toddler boys take naturally to dolls, but adults think that's somehow inappropriate," says John Turner. A preschool teacher at a workshop at Oregon's Chemeketa Community College agrees: "Little boys get the nurturing instinct beat out of them." Squashing the affection, nurturing, and sensitivity out of males, adds Turner, is a particularly North American WASP quality.

By 9 or 10, youngsters begin shifting from toys and imagination to hobbies and applied skills. They begin to view their activities as "recreation" rather than play, but the learning and exploring are as real as in early childhood — perhaps more so. Instead of making pretend cakes from sand, 10 and 11 year olds make real ones in the kitchen; hammers and nails and needles and craft items replace blocks and Legos.

By the early teens, recreation seems as all-consuming as play is for 2-year-olds. By now, youngsters should have acquired some driving, consuming interests. They are able to focus, to concentrate upon perfecting particular skills, and they begin to "get good at" things. They are past toys; now kids need — *need* — realia: a quality microscope, a good camera, a versatile sewing machine, a set of functional shop or mechanic's tools.

All modern theorists except, perhaps, the strictest of Puritans agree: Play is useful, valuable, and necessary. It is the child's laboratory, his applied practice, in experimenting, problem solving, in discovering the natural laws of science and of human behavior, and in social dynamics.

Well, actually, Klingons agree with the Puritans. All pain and no fun. If you've met Lieutenant Worf (*Star Trek: Next Generation*) you've met a man trained to be devoid of humor and compassion, whose major goals in relationships are to outmaneuver and to preserve honor. A man whose whole culture is based on waging conflict but whose major one rages in himself. We feel there's warmth and empathy in there trying to get out, but the cultural man outwillpowers the inate one.

We received an insight to Mr. Worf's hang-ups when he once said scornfully, "*I* . . . did not *play* with toys."

Toys must *do* something. Fire the imagination. Develop coordination, muscles, and movement. Induce kids to build, to create, to manipulate, to learn to control. Provide things to remember, discover, figure out, learn. And lend friendship and companionship: a teddy and blankie are necessary valuables.

Drug, department, dime, and discount stores' toy sections are jammed with things that don't do anything. They are consumer products. If you want to see toys of real educational, emotional, and developmental value, take a whirl through a Toys 'R' Us. The store is a fair-and-exposition of how human mind and muscle develop and grow; if you start out with a vague goal of "getting something that will do him some good" but don't know what *does* do him some good, you can cruise through a Toys 'R' Us and not only find specific things for specific kids, but you can take out enough information to equal a whole three-credit course in Child Development. (Or in Grandma Development. Two Christmases ago, Bob gave me a Toys 'R' Us gift certificate.)

Or attend a Discovery Toys "party." (I have heard parents highly praising Discovery Toys. However, in the interest of balanced journalism, I must add that some of them are Discovery dealers.)

Play has long been used for analyzing what makes a child tick. Through observing a young person at play, psychologists and specifically trained teachers can diagnose social and emotional problems, and utilize play as therapy in treating them. Doing so, however, takes more training and skill than most of us have. The ordinary armchair psychologist's misdiagnoses can't possibly benefit either the youngster or his parents.

What's more important, I think, is that by observing a child at play, we can derive some pretty reliable conclusions as to how he learns, and how he solves problems, interacts, and communicates.

That was one of the things John Turner meant: "As the child plays, so the man shall work."

He also meant that by observing a young person at play — or at recreation — we can predict, to a greater degree than you may have thought, how he will function as an adult. The way the child gets along, forms friendships, plays as a team member. Whether he approaches things with a sense of challenge, or defeat; with enthusiasm, or hostility. Whether he sticks to it and finishes, or frogs from one activity to another. Whether he is careful, or indifferent. Whether he strives, or settles for sloppiness and mediocrity. Whether he plays the game for enjoyment, or

his only criteria is winning. All these are the child at play . . .
the man at work.

So how do you suppose Stan "Thorney" Thorne played
with his teddy bear?

> Young kids call it play; big kids call it
> recreation. It is the means by which kids develop all
> the useful skills, aptitudes, and attitudes they will
> use in adulthood. The 5-year-old at play is the adult
> at work.

38

Free stuff for kids

Some of the best materials for play and learning are simple items you can find for free, and they're also things kids happen to enjoy the most.

Resource persons are happy to provide surplus materials for kids' use. In fact, if you represent a school, pre-school, day care, or youth group, you may procure items some merchants don't ordinarily give away.

WALLPAPER SAMPLE BOOKS — Adventures in texture, color, and patterns. From stores carrying home decorating items. Books are discarded each season, two to four times per year.

LARGE CARTONS — Appliance, electronics, furniture stores; building supply centers. Big boxes spark more creativity than just about anything.

MAGAZINES — Public libraries regularly discard old periodicals as well as worn-out books. Ask your librarian to notify you when it's housecleaning time. Surplus magazines and brochures with pictures may also be available from insurance agents, airlines, churches, and others who distribute in-house magazines to clients.

Try local or regional magazine distributors. Unsold copies are picked up and (usually) destroyed.

BLOCKS, WOOD SCRAPS — Construction sites. Contact builders, request permission to pick up millend blocks and wood scraps. You'll often find zillions of smooth, evenly sized blocks (2" x 2", 2" x 4", 4" x 6" are common sizes).

COLOR CHIPS — From stores selling paint, floor and counter covering.

CARPET REMNANTS — Samples and bolt-ends of discontinued patterns from floor covering retailers.

FABRIC AND DECORATIVES — Cloth remnants, yarn, odd buttons, artsy-craftsy items from stores selling fabric, notions, and craft materials.

PAPER — End of bolt, odd sizes, print overruns, other throwaway paper, from photocopy centers, print shops, computer stores and places conducting computer classes.

PROMOTIONALS — Balloons, pencils, scratch pads, and other items with promo logos from banks, auto dealers, insurance agents.

39

Education doesn't make any difference

News item: In a survey of 220 teenagers, 81 percent of them said they spend their weekends in the sun. Only 9 percent use sunscreen.

Survey question: Do you know the dangers of sun on the skin?

Survey answer: Yes.

In the early eighties, my school's second period biology class conducted a survey of its own. Every student present filled out the questionnaire, one hundred percent participation. The biology teacher even taught her students to compute the margin of error, which she explained as "the goof-off factor." Surveyees fib, she told the kids.

The questions: Have you ever smoked marajuana? How often? How many joints a week do you smoke?

For the rest of the day, the kids were a-buzz. This time, school had actually connected to their lives, involved them. *Surely this is more important at the moment than descriptive paragraphing. Let the kids at it — they won't concentrate on grammar, anyway.* I asked a few, and I listened.

"Adjusting for the the goof-off factor," a junior told me, "eighty-five percent of the kids in Riverbank High toke grass. "

"The preacher's kid wrote that he smokes ten joints a week," one boy scoffed. "What a liar. Guys like that mess up our statistical validity." A classmate countered that the P.K. "just talked big so he didn't feel like such an oddball."

"I wouldn't name anyone who does toke," another teased me. "But I know all six of the kids who don't. You want to know?"

"Naaahh," I said. "Then I might have to lie under oath if the Feds ever come to torture the truth out of me... By the way, guys. Haven't you been watching the news? About the effects of grass? It fries your brain, destroys your health, leads to hard stuff, and you gentlemen . . . well . . . you know. "

Abruptly, the climate changed. "That's all preaching," said a boy whose smile suddenly tightened. "By do-goodies who don't like teen-agers."

"They haven't absolutely proven marajuana has any harmful effects," said another. "It's just scare talk."

Regardless of what is ever conclusively proven — about anything — there are always those who uphold one's right to destroy himself, I thought grimly. Like civil libertarians and the tobacco lobby. It gives people the option to glom on to whatever they want to believe.

"Well, one thing has been proven," I said. "Drugs are illegal."

"A lot of things are illegal. But we do them. Darcy's brother steals from the store and my old man makes beer and lets me drink it."

After school, when the teachers gathered, I said sadly, "Some days I wonder if we're doing any good at all. Education doesn't seem to make any difference."

A couple of years later Darcy's brother became another statistic in the biggest epidemic of suicide Alaska had ever seen.

An Oregon mother filed child molestation charges against a thirtyish man. Her daughter, age 9, appeared before the county grand jury to tell what happened as she recalled it.

"Me and Marcy were swinging at the park and this man with a beard came up to us and said he'd give us some candy. He took us in the trees and gave us candy bars. Then he took our jeans and panties down and played with us and stuff."

"Did you like that?" a grandmotherly juror asked gently.

The little girl smiled winsomely and nodded. "Yes."

"Then what happened?" asked a gentleman of the jury.

"Then he took out his thing and let us touch it and then me and Marcy got up and ran."

The jurors knew that these girls had, within the past month, been exposed to education on this topic. The public schools in that city had just completed an awareness/anti-abuse course, taught in every grade, 1 through 12. It had been the subject of considerable controversy. Some citizens felt strongly that such did not belong in the public schools; others were equally convinced that the topic was so important it should be taught both at school and at home, each reinforcing the other.

Knowing this, a juror asked, "Has your mother told you not to go anywhere with a strange man?"

The smile again. "Yes."

"Did they tell you that in school, too?"

"Yes."

"Why did you go with him?"

The child shrugged and smiled. "We wanted to."

After the little girl left, a silent, gray pall shrouded the jury chamber. Finally the grandmother, a school bus driver who spent many hours a week with children, spoke in a tone of mingled frustration, anger, and sadness. "Education doesn't make any difference."

It doesn't seem to make much difference to anyone, youth or adult. In 1991, 131 new cereals were introduced to America, says *Consumer Report*, and 85 percent of them were 50 percent-sugar confections targeted to children. In school cafeterias, nitrate, fat, salt, and sugar still prevail, and dieticians aid and abet the kids' malnutritive habits, saying if they don't serve them at school the kids go to the nearest market and buy them there. The number of fetal alcohol syndrome and crack babies continues to increase annually: in some hospitals one-quarter of newborns are addicts at birth.

Do people not know? Sure, they know.

Is knowing a deterrent? Of course not.

If one thing is available in America, it is education; if one thing is sacred, it is the public's right to know. "They" keep insisting that people do not. "The masses of people have no access to information," *they* claim.

Excuse me. People seem able to find out what they want to know. Where to buy, how to fence. The title and artist of the latest controversial rock, rap, and video. What's free and who's easy.

The forgivers try another excuse. "People can't read," *they* say.

Pardon me again. If they can't read, what do they *do* with all those magazines and papers at the checkstands?

What people do not do is apply what they know.

So we continue to overextend ourselves financially and we leave valuables in cars locked or unlocked.

We say this nation absolutely has to Throw The Rascals Out, then we vote them back in.

We buy leaded crystal stemware because it is so sparkly and glamorous and looks so upscale in the ads. We say Just This Once Won't Hurt Anything; we challenge the brake shoes to last another thousand miles, and we start over the mountains without tire chains.

The elderly get ripped off, time after time, in scam after scam, and we brush it off, forgiving: "They have no way of knowing." Society forgives all who do not know: children, teens, the inexperienced, the old; the undereducated, language-barriered, disabled, unemployed, unaffluent, the stressed-out, the laid-back. Who is left to be accountable?

This is not one of those "This is the problem And this is what we can do about it" pieces, because I do not know what to do about it, and please pass the chips and beer and don't preach unproven scare talk when you do.

> Parents ... scientists ... writers ... teachers: Why are we doing this? Our agony is: so little of it makes any difference.

40

Relating to the peer group

"From infancy on, he related well to adults," a dad said. "He never talked baby talk, and his thinking process was advanced for his age. We saw it as an advantage. Until junior high. Then a counselor said he 'doesn't relate to his peer group' and he was called maladjusted."

When he was 18 he went to work. Immediately, he got on the right side of the boss and his coworkers. "He isn't like other young people starting out," the boss once told the dad. "Most youngsters don't know how to get along outside of the youth culture. He came here already knowing how to relate to adults, and that gives him an enormous advantage over his peers."

When Liz was nine, her teachers labeled her. "Too adult. A social loner. Not properly adjusted to childhood." During her high school years, Liz became a marvellous cook, learned computer programming, wrote fiction, and spent hundreds of hours debating philosophy and world affairs with her graduate-degreed parents.

During her first term at Arizona State, Liz became the youngest assistant counselor her dorm had ever hired and, said the head resident, one of the best. "She has an adult outlook; she approaches problems and counsels students with maturity," said the H.R.

"We never had a generation gap," Liz's mother said. "We've always been her peer group."

"Well-meaning grown-ups are too quick to call a child abnormal," the boy's dad said. "We are adults longer than we are children, and for most of our lives, it never matters that we didn't boogie with the kids."

41

Till Eulenspiegel

The first quarter of my sophomore year in college, I signed up for brass class. I did it because that's what music majors did: they took class instruction in brass, woodwind, percussion, string instruments, and piano — all of them. If you already played a brass instrument, you learned another. So I took up French horn. There's always a shortage of French horns, a player is always in demand. Why not be in demand? Learn a trade that has a job market.

I got along with the horn, and there was a demand, indeed. Before the end of the quarter I transferred from the overpopulated trombone barrio (I knew all those guys real well by then, so why not branch out?) to an impoverished horn section. It was nice to be needed.

I was assigned to third horn, which is the easiest French horn line. This was not a put-down: I knew what I could not do, and so did Dr. Christiansen. The Central Washington College of Education Concert Band of 1954-55 was a cracking good one, and to be allowed to play anything at all in it was accomplishment enough. The program for our winter concert tour was packed with muscle and weight. I practiced like crazy so I could cut the stuff.

The second day of the tour, Andy, our first hornist, conked out on us.

"Okay," Dr. Chris said. "Darlene, you take first; Susan, go to second; Dennis, stay on fourth. We'll leave third uncovered." Third horn is not only the easy line, it's the dispensible one. Chris swept the three of us with a swivel of his huge brown eyes. "And you guys . . . stay . . . *awake!*" Interperetation: Do it right or flunk.

I tried not to strangle. "Darlene, I can't do this!" I croaked.

"Sure, you can," she said calmly.

She was right. At the end of the second selection, I whispered, "I can't believe this. I'm playing way past my limit."

"People can do more than they think," she said, still calm. "Me, too."

When Andy took ill, Chris told his bandsmen, "We'll scratch *Till Eulenspiegel.*" Richard Strauss's *Till Eulenspiegel's Merry Pranks* is a brilliant, showy piece containing one of the best known, and most difficult, French horn passages in music literature. It isn't for just any hornist. No Andy — no *Till.*

If Darlene and I were playing over our heads, so was everyone else. Buoyed by our brilliant performances, perhaps, Chris jauntily took us through warm-up for the morning concert of the third day. It was his custom to plan each program about ten seconds in advance. He would take the podium and bow to the audience, and while they applauded he would turn to us and snap out the title of the next number to be played.

This morning he bowed, they applauded, and then he turned and said crisply, "*Till Eulenspiegel!*" — he said it with an exclamation mark. He turned and bowed again, and maybe over the applause he did not hear his band's collective gasp. Darlene did not gasp. She semi-smiled as she calmly arranged the score on her stand.

Well, let me tell you. That girl played some horn. If you closed your eyes you'd have sworn that was Andy Setlow playing those merry pranks. Even the woodwinds, most of whom dreaded the piece because . . . it's . . . tough! — even they played as never before. Success is an epidemic thing.

As the final chord reverberated, Chris spun around and, before they could start clapping, he raised a gangly arm toward the band and said, "Our French horn soloist: Miss Darlene Brown of Leavenworth, Washington." Chris motioned Darlene to stand, and as she rose, so did the audience. An ovation. Then the CWSC Concert Band joined in the applause and I was chilly all over.

Later, on the bus, I asked Darlene, "Did you know you were going to play that?"

"Uh-uh."

"Weren't you scared?"

"Uh-uh." Thoughtful pause. "You can always do more than you think. You just don't get enough chances to find out." Her eyes sparkled. "Anyway, Chris told me he heard me playing it in the practice room last week."

"Somehow . . . this is going to make both of us better teachers," I told her.

Then I went to the back of the bus to play pinochle, and I played against trumpeter Harley Brumbaugh, who grew up to become one of the Northern Hemisphere's most eminent musicians, and my side lost.

> "You can always do more than you think.
> You just don't get enough chances to find out."
> — *Darlene Brown*

42

Monarchs, standing in the shade

The Class of Eighty-One was the kind of group people have in mind when they think they want to become teachers. The 81'ers had only one downside: They were going to graduate.

"I'm losing half the horsepower in my band," I fretted. "The newspaper will go away."

"I won't have a yearbook photographer," moaned the adviser.

"We may as well skip volleyball next year," lamented the coach.

It didn't happen that way. It was as if the second- and third-best trumpet players and clarinetists and flutists had been waiting for the reigning monarchs to leave, too timid, perhaps, to tread on someone else's ground, or maybe they were unable to bloom in the shade. Coming up through the ranks of obscure freshmen and sophomores were reporters and photographers and artists, actors, and athletes still unrecognized, not yet tapped.

In 1982 everything our small high school did was done better than any year before; and after that, things improved. When I finally left, along with the Class of 84, we had the volleyball champs and the district's best band; a yearbook of such quality that other schools thought we had ours professionally made up; and our school fishwrapper, still produced by typewriter and ditto machine, scooped a statewide newspaper on the most important Native Alaskan meeting of the year.

That the earth still turned and the moon still rose after the 81ers walked away shouldn't have been such a surprise, given the number of times I have survived We Can't Survive Without Her/ Him/ Them.

When I was a freshman in high school . . . the band again . . . *Thee* solo cornet and several of *Thee* others graduated. *Next year will be awful; maybe I'll be embarrassed to be here.* Then: *No. After they're gone, I'll have a chance to shine.* Obviously, quite a few other kids were waiting for their chances to shine, too— because we did.

I figured that after I graduated, the band would go downhill, probably be so bad the music teacher would resign and go to another county. Twenty-five years later another band man who taught near my hometown in my era told me, "Ilwaco High School had a SCREAMING GOOD band in . . . " — and he called off the year after I graduated, and two or three years after that. My old band screamed without me. With my old music teacher still in charge, of course.

When you are a newcomer to a group, you step in knowing there's a certain ranking, a pecking order. A status, which, when you're new on the block, you'd better leave quo. When I started college, a senior named Russ was the Reigning Monarch Of The Trombones. The first week of the following year, after Russ had graduated, another 'boner, a junior named Don Goodale, started doing amazing things with that piece of plumbing he played.

"Goodale, how come you didn't do that flashy stuff last year?" I asked in awe.

"Last year the bone section was Russ's," Goodale answered.

From those experiences I have learned that replacements are always available, that talent is always waiting in the wings, waiting for its opportunity to step out of someone else's shadow. And from *Till Eulenspiegel* I learned that people are capable of more than they thought, if only they find an opportunity to discover what and how much it is.

In my high school classes there were always those few dominants, just as it is with any group of people of any age in any setting. Taking charge, they take over. Leading a discussion, they monopolize. Serving on a committee . . . forget the committee.

Now, I acknowledge that the prevailing educational thought of the time is to stack classes homogeneously: each class, each "project," each discussion group contains a bright, a slow; an articulate, an illiterate; an expressive, a reticent; a timid, a vavoom . . . you get the idea.

For homogeneous grouping, there are two theories at work. One is educational: when you integrate, the accomplished feed and the underachievers are fed. The other is the deal about political correctness. The important discovery I have made about integrating multiple levels of intellect/achievement/personality is: It doesn't work. Kids do not challenge Reigning Monarchs.

So I began practicing de-integration in my high school classes. I placed the kids in preordained groups (that means they were assigned, non-negotiable) and gave each group a specific task with a definite deadline.

First, the groups had to be small. Two or three, so that each individual *had* to participate, to be accountable. If you've ever worked on a committee, or if you've observed the U.S. Congress in action, you understand the advantage here.

Second, the Reigning Monarchs were grouped together, made to slug it out.

Third, the kids who were recognized as non-achieving non-leaders were given the chance to . . . *ACHIEVE!* And achieve they did. They surprised themselves, astounded the Monarchs (whose earliest assignments ended in futile, fruitless impasse; they learned to work it through), amazed the other teachers, and gratified the administrator. The only one who wasn't surprised was myself. I would not have risked the kids' self-esteem if I had not been absolutely certain this was going to work.

Near the end of my first year of college I began thinking, again, about students graduating, about how the world as I knew it would change. What this school is, I thought, is the people who are here right now. When the seniors leave, this college will be only a fragment of itself and not the real thing. I thought about transferring, moving to a school that was intact. But I had gone through the shopping around, the applying, the admissioning once. I guessed I didn't really want to do it all again. I returned.

I never missed the gone grads; I seldom even thought of them. New stars had waited in the wings and they shone brighter than the ones forgotten.

It was that remembrance I kept when my husband and I were about to leave the school district where we had been for over twenty years. People were very kind. "We'll miss you," they said. "It will never be the same here we can't possibly get along without you we'll remember you always."

Those were gracious epithets, but I knew that in a couple of years we'd be forgotten. We were. The Christmas cards fell off to a handful, and then, four or five years later, we met some teachers who had gone to the area we left. "Henrys?" they pondered. "Hmmmm, don't think I ever heard the name."

For anyone who works with kids, there are two important lessons here. They may appear contradictory but they are not.

1 — Inside of every youngster are talent and competence, rattling chains and roaring to get out. It may be a matter of time and place, or of someone stepping away and letting the person out of the shade; or it may be a matter of being given a push, shove, and an opportunity, which is up to you to do.

2 — When the person becomes the best there is, someone else will follow and do it better. We hope, we aspire, we achieve. And we realize our monarchy is mortal.

5

The Complete Person

Full bloom

Joey Novak 7/87/

43

Creativity: The highest level

"Creativity is the highest level of thought." Those are the words of Jean Piaget, the Swiss psychologist whose studies of how young children think and develop are the standards of measure.

The word "creative" and its derivatives have become maligned words in our language. Here, we do not mean creative as in Creative Participatory Enhancement (user fee), Creative Product Image Projection (advertising that persuades consumers they need unnecessary things), or Creative Contingency Rationale (a teenager's alibi for getting home late).

Here, creativity is the expression of the inner person through art and ideas. It is a product of environment, intellect, soul, and senses. In form and quality it varies with the time of the world, the mood of the producer, the perception of the beholder. It is a blend of the concrete and abstract, the utilitarian and aesthetic, of intuition, logic, and the inexplicable. Its omega is a product shared with anyone who wants it but its alpha is the inner drive of the one who creates it. Creativity, along with the use of tools and language, sets us apart from other lifeforms and distinguishes us as human.

We seek to foster creativity because that is the expression of our individuality. It is what makes human beings adaptable . . . survivable.

We think of creativity as being art and The Arts, and part of it is. The artist confronts and solves problems of space and place, utilizing movement, perception, and academics: math and science and coordination and visual acuity.

The artist, the musician, actor, writer: they take empty air and blank spaces and turn them into meaningful sights and sounds and expressions and emotions, and do it within prescribed technical frameworks.

But creativity is more than art. It is any form of original problem solving; of making things from other things or from nothing; of coping and managing and handling. Creativity is a high achievement because it must involve all the thought processes, all the academic and developmental disciplines. It combines what is known with what is felt: fact with intuition. It spawns original sights, sounds, movements, ideas. It blends knowledge with conjecture and solves problems, finds answers, suggests options and alternatives.

It's an attitude. The difference between spending a lifetime looking for happiness for yourself, or radiating outward until you come to realize that the only way to happiness is to create joy for others, whether it's to make them laugh, propagate a new flower, to heal, or throw a coat over a puddle for someone else to step on.

"Young children are creative by nature," says Thomas Armstrong, educational psychologist and learning specialist at the National Parenting Center. It's up to the adults in charge to "keep that creativity alive."

The biggest zinger to nurturing creativity is that so much of the tools of creativity are spendy. It requires materials and space. We aren't saying go out and buy an orchestra and we aren't saying enroll the kids in every class available or build an addition on your house. Schools *should* be helping you out, providing materials and instruction; but in tight times, the creative disciplines are generally the first to go (right after the counselor).

Many communities offer magnificent kids' programs, thanks to local councils of the arts or individual galleries, the public library, YWCA, municipal Parks and Recreation, summer day camps, and the like.

There is a definite place for puzzles, follow-the-dots, kits for constructing things according to directions and diagrams, remote controlled and mechanical widgets, and games with rules; and it helps if you are aware of the purposes of such items. However, they do not foster creativity.

Many children have the potential for high creative achievement. It may be apparent early. Some aptitudes may not emerge until adolescence, even adulthood. Do not expect, and do not push for prodigy quality.

Sure, everyone knows Mozart composed a symphony at four. You know it because it's extraordinary — it made the news. We said your child is naturally creative; we didn't say he's a natural-born genius.

If your kids turn out to be highly creative, there's something you should know. Creative people are Aquarian, whether they're born Aquarius or not. Intelligent, but sensitive . . . moody, quirky. You know the popular stereotypes — the eccentric artist, the weird musician, the mad scientist, the writer possessed. Well, it's all true. Ho, boy, is it ever.

How to foster creativity

❑ Nurture your own creativity. In doing so, you set examples, provide patterns. You demonstrate that making things and making up things are worthwhile. Equally, you continue to nurture yourself as a person.

❑ Go along with the child's imagination. If there's a dinosaur in the living room . . . there's a dinosaur! Escape its reach if the child directs you to. Remind the youngster that the alien in your house, whatever it is, is friendly and playful. If it isn't, the child will either convert it or overcome it.

❑ Provide raw materials, and the time and space to use them. Paper, paste, bits of fabric, yarn, rickrack; music for moving and singing; blocks, scraps of wood. Story books and pictures. Sand and dirt and realia to discover things about the world and the laws of science. Dress-up clothes and other props for dramatic play.

❑ Not inducive to creating and imagining: Anything that does things by itself (the child is not in control, the *thing* is), anything that is not interactive (things he cannot respond to).

❑ Praise, encourage, and take pride in the child's efforts, whatever the efforts and whatever his age. Don't issue negative judgments. Do acknowledge his ideas and products.

Problem solving and creativity

Use what you know and what you can do, and do what has to be done with whatever things you have at hand to do it with.

Restated, simpler: Figure out what has to be done and how to do it. Then do it.

Let kids figure it out themselves. . . No, *make* them.

Every time a child grapples and wins, he grows. Every time someone else does it for him, he shrinks.

There are limits, of course. The child's knowledge and experience. His maturity and inate ability. The time and patience it takes to wait him out to arrive at a solution and act on it. The number of adults available who can wait and encourage, and the number of other children around who are getting into trouble while *they* wait.

Adults are likely to jump in too quickly and bail a child out too often. What he learns then is not to grapple but to stall, and every time he stalls he atrophies.

There's a fine line between shielding a child from destructive levels of frustration and stress, and creating a pattern of cop-out. There's a breathlessly short space between nudging him upward and pushing him down. And for that, we don't have any easy solutions.

44

Conformity and drumsticks

By ANDREA CRAIN

Andrea Crain, a 15-year-old writer-to-be at Francis Howell High School, St. Charles, Missouri, challenges teenagers to dare to be nonconformists. Like so many people who are dedicated creatives, Andrea says she is known to her fellow students as "an individualist — maybe a little odd," and that doesn't make her feel odd at all. In fact, she says, she cherishes her individuality.

The pressure to conform can weigh heavily on the shoulders of a creative young person. It may come from friends who don't like big words, parents who think art is impractical, or any number of other sources. If you are good at something, you may not show it because you don't want to stand out.

A little bit of conforming may not damage your identity. Too much pressure to march to the regulation drumbeat, on the other hand, could do you more harm than good. It might cause stress or a lack of self esteem. It may create friendships which only rest on shallow foundations. Talent may lay untapped.

The pressure of being yourself may be no more than a minor irritation if you choose to run down your very own path. You will find it's more interesting to be like no one but yourself.

If you aren't doing something that you want because it's not normal, perhaps you should ask yourself, "What is normal?"

Oddity can be a great deal of fun. Just look at all the people who go to science fiction conventions or dye their hair purple. The "normal" majority would find this highly irregular and quite unacceptable. Those persons are unwilling to break out of the good-old standard mold. They are missing a lot if their molds are not of a shape they truly like.

If you discover you don't really know what you've been working for, go ahead . . . shatter the mold. Pick up your drumsticks and tap out a jazzy beat. Do whatever and as much as you're capable of.

Most of all, enjoy yourself.

45

Music

My car was full of granddaughters. An almost-two, a just-turned-two, and a four. (That's a car full.) Spontaneously, as if on cue, the little girls burst into song. *Twinnnkle, twinnnkle little staarr . . . Old MacDonald had a farm . . .*

Abruptly and at the same time, they stopped. They looked at one another, and at me, in delighted surprise. "Grandma! She knows the same songs we do!" the four-year-old Oregonian said of her California cousin, the almost-two. "And you do, too!"

Music, the universal language. At least they once said that, though it was always a sweeping overstatement. There have always been ethnic differences, where "they" do not understand "our" music; and now there are huge chasms between the music of generations, where we definitely do not understand.

(Our language calls all rhythm and intonation by the name Music. We have Classical Theatre, Melodrama, and Stand-Up Comics. We have Novels, Poetry, and Journalism; and Painting, Sculpture, and Photography. Yet we toss Rachmaninoff, the Tabernacle Choir, and Dirty Acid Five all together and call it all music. We need a new name for sounds like DAF; and for its performers, a designation other than the word Artists.)

Children are innately musical. There is evidence that a six-month fetus hears and responds to music. Babies are born with a sense of rhythm. Rhythms stimulate infants to activity or repose, to agitation or calmness. Without coaching or example, babies set feet, arms, and bodies to the movements we call dancing, and rhythmical movement is common to all cultures. Rhythmical improvisation may be the human's first creative expression.

The love of song is likewise inherent. Little children vocalize in pitches and cadences before they can talk; they can sing short songs before they speak sentences. Eventually singing becomes an intensely personal thing, and sooner or later most children enter a phase where they stop singing solo. I think they feel that singing reveals too much of their private selves, just as people feel about praying in public or reading their own poetry.

How to tell if youngsters are musically talented

❑ The talented possess a stronger, more compelling interest in music, songs, and rhythms than their age mates.

❑ Interest is sustained throughout the middle grades, when less endowed youngsters tend to give it up.

❑ Around 9, 11, the talented will probably want to begin learning an instrument.

❑ By 5 or 6, he carries a tune well. By 8 or 10, demonstrates a "good voice" and begins singing harmonies.

❑ By age 3 or 4, the musically interested listens attentively and studiously to a variety of kinds and styles of music, and by 10 or 12, may listen to analyze it rather than merely to be entertained.

❑ Be careful and judicious, though, to distinguish whether a child is truly interested in music; or whether he listens to what's popular because it's the popular thing to do. Don't confuse Pounding On Drums with serious interest in an art that requires discipline and work.

Children constitute a significant segment of American consumers. Business recognizes that. There is far and away more kid music out there now than in the eighties. Some of it is amateurish, poorly done, and just simply bad — someone's obvious attempt to cash in on a growth industry.

What's "good kiddie music"? Individual judgement of "good" and "bad" is as varied as individuals are, of course; but here we're talking about role models and artistic development.

SELECTING FOR KID-LISTENING:

— Singers should sing with clarity ("chipmunk" types do not) and intonation — in pitch, on key. (Burl Ives, once the flagbearer of children's singers, has serious intonation problems in his later recordings.) A substantial portion of pop country-Western singers who occupy so many places on the dial don't carry tunes any better than you do.

But it's okay if *you* can't carry a tune in a bucket. The difference is that *you* are participating with the child and dee-jays are not. A child can listen to an adult moan and wail through "Twinkle, Twinkle" and then come up with the real melody as it is supposed to be. (Maybe that explains how teens can pick a tune out of a Dirty Acid Five piece.) On the other hand, when you *buy* music (or find it on the radio dial) for kids (or anyone), find the exemplary.

— Arrangements need a range of instrumental and vocal pitches and colors. Piano, guitar, woodwinds, strings. Some ears do not pick up high frequencies, some cannot hear the very low.

— For young children, the more participatory it is, the better. Singing along is participatory, and so is responding actively — marching, moving, imagining-along. (*If you're happy and you know it clap your hands . . . Eensie weensie spider climbed up . . .*) Sesame Street cassettes get kids activated, and so does the *Let's Sing* series.

— Public libraries carry sizable collections on cassettes, with a substantial portion of toddletime tunes accompanied by songbooks or storybooks. It's a convenient, cost-free way to expose youngsters to a vast variety of musical styles and artists.

— For adolescents, music, more than any other catalyst including their hormones, can lead to introspection and touch profound sensibility and emotion which they may not even be able to articulate. These, which you can probably obtain at your library, are particularly getting-in-touch-withs:

Richard Strauss: *An Alpine Symphony;* and *Death and Transfiguration.*

Beethoven: Fourth movement (*Ode to Joy*), Symphony #9; and just about anything, especially if you're feeling broody.

Tchaikovsky: *1812 Overture; Pathètique Symphony* (#6); *The Nutcracker;* the Finale, *Symphony #5.*

Dvorak: Largo movement, *New World Symphony* (#9).

Wagner: *Ride of the Valkyries; Elsa's Procession to the Cathedral;* and everything else, especially *Tannhauser* and *Lohengrin.* (Not the soprano arias, just the instrumentals.)

Haydn: *Hornsignal Overture.*

Neil Diamond: *Taproot Manuscript.*

Simon & Garfunkle: The album, *Concert in Central Park.*

In our zeal to expose kids to making music, we are inclined to buy them "toy" instruments — little one-octave xylophones and plinky pianos, three-dollar "tonette" type wind instruments and three-string toy guitars. Basically, they're no good. Their intonation is terrible and their tone is unendurable. If a child becomes attuned to those sounds, he may never develop a discriminating ear; the imprint is that awful is good enough.

You and the children will do better if you invest in one or two better quality items — in a multi-child household, they'll be passed around, anyway. Try a real guitar — basic, no-frills, and small, but real. At second-hand stores or pawnshops for under $30. Or an in-tune songflute or recorder. (Go for an alto or baritone, for a tonal range you can stand to listen to!) If you can play a keyboard enough to provide guidance with even one finger, spring for a small electronic for your kids. For under $80 you can find keyboards with true pitch and pleasing tone quality, and they are real instruments.

For the smallest musicians, basic rhythm instruments provide performance satisfaction with no sour notes. Try a triangle, tambourine, maracas, or a variety of drum you can stand (like an oatmeal box!). Yes, those things can bring about rambunction . . . but we already said music is a discipline.

For a pre-schooler to play his own cassettes, the market offers toy tape players — which is another "why bother" item.

Real cassette players with real tone cost hardly more than tin ones, so why not surround your kids with the tone and quality of the real thing.

The greatest influence on your children's earliest taste and choice of music, both listening and participating, is your own example. (At least until they discover what "all the kids" are listening to. Then the choice is no longer yours or your youngster's, but the peer group's.) Just as a child's palate gets used to, then develops a preference for, the foods served at home, his tastes in music are influenced by what he hears in earliest childhood. Via radio and stereo, most homes have music in the background much of the time, subliminally, largely without comment. Since tastes and preferences and quality judgments are very individual and very subjective, we'll skip the obvious analogy about junk food for the ears.

When you do choose music, though, whether as background or for participation, be aware: music creates its own psychology and physiology. Rhythm and harmony create moods and metabolism; music fires mind and muscle. It can soothe the savage beast. Or activate it.

Parent recommended music for kids

To find out what's the best in young people's music, we surveyed parents across the U.S. Okay, we talked to some musicians, and we used a computer bulletin board . . . probably no less scientific than a lot of the "surveys" which determine all those Lists Of Best Things.

Exemplary artists: Good news! Some of the favorite artists of your youth are now acclaimed as some of the best for your youngsters. Look for children's albums by ANNE MURRAY, JOE SCRUGGS, GLENN YARBROUGH (you won't enjoy if you have perfect pitch), PETER, PAUL, & MARY (d.b.a. *Peter, Paul, and Mommy*), OLIVIA NEWTON JOHN, PETE SEEGER, PAUL SIMON.

Other dependable-quality favorites: TAJ MAHAL, FRED PENNER, KEVIN ROTH, PETER ALSOP, RAFFI, SESAME STREET productions, WALT DISNEY soundtracks.

Not just for kids but exemplary stuff for all: LINDA RONSTADT and JOAN BAEZ have mellowed and matured; their 1990s voices outshine what you heard in your youth. LADYSMITH BLACK MAMBAZO, if you want to find out what the human voice can do, and SWEET HONEY IN THE ROCK, Ladysmith's approximate female counterpart group. BOSTON POPS playing just about anything.

Recommended albums and series: LET'S SING series (Metacom, Plymouth, MN).

SONGS FOR LITTLE ANGELS WITH DIRTY FACES, with accompanying songbooks available (Sonos Music Resources, Orem, UT).

KIDSONGS (Klutz Studio, Palo alto).

EARTHBEAT! series, the power and soul of many cultures and traditions, recorded by authentic ethnic artists.

MISSA LUBA, by Muungano National Choir of Kenya.

CLASSICAL KIDS — Story lines and narratives on a series of four cassettes acquaint kids with Mozart, Bach, Vivaldi, Beethoven. Optional and additional are notebooks with activities for adults and kids.

Neil Diamond's TAPROOT MANUSCRIPT endures.

FAMILY FOLK FESTIVAL is 42 minutes of African and Western Hemisphere sing-along folk by the prestigious artists of their cultures. Most SESAME STREET productions are good; some have sloppy musicianship and patronizing-voiced adults, obviously cashing in on the wave.

Videos: KIDSONGS series— all the familiar songs of childhood, plus classics of the American heritage, in a truly interactive style; it's impossible to remain a potato-viewer with these.

Disney's FANTASIA— combines awe inspiring art, fine classical music interpretations and marvellous language/ imagination jumpstarters, and without a lot of adult chatter.

THE SNOWMAN— superb, sensitive hand drawn art with an outstanding score provides a perfect setting for children of all ages to narrate their own story. WEE SING vids apparently sell well, but to our experts, their silliness and dumb acting are without artistic merit.

Good place to find most of what you're looking for: MUSIC FOR LITTLE PEOPLE catalog (Box 1460, Redway, CA 99560. Catalog is free and so is the call, 1-800-346-4445).

"Commercially popular" cartoons, a la $6.95 vids and Saturday mornings: For value-model characters, story lines, musical backgrounds, and artistic impression, our critics unanimously agree: Thumbs Down.

"But kids like them!" . . . Well, we like bacon and eggs and playing the slots, but . . .

46

Art

She's so creative. *Yes, she draws such lovely pictures.*

He's very expressive. *Yes, you can tell by the way he uses lines and color.*

We are selecting kids for our school's Talented and Gifted program. *Norman and Linson are outstanding sketchers, and Tom does gorgeous woodcuts.*

Art — drawing, painting, carving, making things that are decorative and esthetically pleasing — is by no means the definition of creativity, expression, talent, or giftedness; but it's usually the first discipline that comes to mind when you say the words. Of all the realms of creativity, art is probably the most utilized by the most people as a spare-time endeavor. We all sketch and scratch and doodle, and everyone tries a hand at figures and pictures; and it's the one most likely to be self-developed. Without benefit of lessons or formal training, many a fine artist has become.

Sometime during your grade schooling, they explained to you that art is one of humankind's most valuable assets because it has recorded so much of human history.

Teacher: We know our prehistoric forebears dined on mammoth and sabretooth because prehistoric caves are illustrated with pictures of the hunt.

Student: *So did Arthurians barbecue dragons and Nessies?*

T: Dinosaurs were blue and green. *We say they are because the first artists drew them that way, and now everyone makes blue and green dinosaurs. And purple. Brontosaurus is purple.*

Did ancient Egyptians come only in profile?

Jesus was Jewish. Why does he look Italian? Because his first portrait was made during the Renaissance, and Renaissance painters were Italian. *He always looks skinny and gangly, with Jergens-lotion hands. If he was a carpenter and fisherman, and he did all his traveling on foot, wouldn't he be calloused and sunburned and muscular?* Renaissance painters were courtesans, and courtesans were kind of wimpy. (This conversation does not take place in a public school, of course. Only at a place where kids are allowed to mention Jesus, even if it's only a matter of historical or artistic curiosity.)

Mom: Our house doesn't look like that. Why do you draw our house with a triangular roof and the door right in the middle? *Because that's the way I draw a house.*

M: I haven't worn a dress in three years. How come you always draw me with a dress? *Because kids depict females in a dress. A stick figure with a triangle. It's universal, across time and cultures.*

Scenario: A three, four, five, eight-year-old is drawing. A grownup intervenes.

"That's not what it looks like . . . That's not how you make it. . . Not neat, Wrong color, Careless, Lines aren't straight . . ."

Or the child gets frustrated. "It doesn't look like it's supposed to; Can't make an elephant's trunk; You can't tell what it is, I can't draw as well as Sandy, This is no good, I'm no good." Tears, rage, disappointment.

From what I've seen over the years, when little children engage in something artistic, it's just another time for family friction, worse than going to the zoo. We forget, and so they do, too, that what's important is the process — the trying, the experimenting, dabbling, messing. Not the product.

Even at the primitive-trial stage, some kids realize their product isn't well done, or recognizable, or "good." But not always. When I was little-tiny, I must have thought whatever I did or made was passable, because when I was in second grade, I was puzzled about how-come my mom didn't have my works of art hung or displayed, the way the other kids' moms had theirs. Unfortunately, I asked.

"Because I won't have that crap cluttering up my house," she said. That pretty much ended my artist's life.

Friction and criticism aren't applied so much to older kids. Those who survive the squashing-it-out stage usually do so either because they are inately talented, or they're dedicatedly interested. The 10 or 12-year-old or the teenager who produces a pleasing product receives praise and applause, which fuels the fire within and encourages him upward.

A child's art does not reflect what he *feels* so much as it shows what he can *do*. He can produce only in tune with his own individual development of his own neuromotor system — the synchronization of mind, muscle, movement, and maturation. There's a sequence.

— The infant first holds his head up, then voluntarily moves his shoulders as he does when he turns over. Then the upper chest, to lift himself up when on his stomach. By the first birthday, he can control upper arm movements.

— Around a year and a half he gains control of the arm to the elbow. He can make sweeping arcs with a crayon.

— By 2 1/2, most kids have enough wrist control to make circular motions but NOT "good circles" — certainly not exact enough ones to please their dads.

— "Good circles" shouldn't be expected until the child approaches 4. Kids love circles and spirals. The reason? From ancient times, a circle has been a symbol of The Self. (The Egyptians' circles weren't so much the sun per se, but their belief that humans are descendents of the sun; thus, themselves.) To 3-year-olds, the circle *is* a person, complete as it stands, without having to add arms and legs.

— Between 5 and 6, kids gain control of the fingertips. Then they are able to begin drawing finer movements (including letters and numerals) and figures with symmetry and proportion.

Just as we may try to derive too much historical fact from pictures, we extract far too much psychoanalysis about kids from their drawings. Take the matter of black.

"Oh, my Jesus," says Mom. (Teacher wouldn't say that because T. can't speak the name in public school.) "She's using *all* that BLACK." Black is supposed to mean disturbed. I have known parents and teachers who tossed the black crayons, no kidding, so the youngsters wouldn't look like disturbed children.

Black is *not* disturbed. It's practical. It's emphatic. Look at cartoons, comic papers, coloring books, and illustrations in the Newberry-Medaled, Caldecott-Awarded children's books. Pictures are outlined, clear and bold, in black. *Words* are black: on signs, in the mail, on cereal boxes, and in the books kids read. In formal and business circles, black is still the correct color for written words to be.

Black is poetic. It's silhouette and shadow, the lash that winks in merriment, the musical note, the cat and dog, the sky that forms the backdrop for the Dipper and the moonlight. Black is elegance: the long, sleek, extravagant luxury car the moonlight shimmers on, and the five thousand dollar velvet gown standing beside it.

Black is dramatic, emphatic, positive, self-assured.
Put the black crayon back and let kids use it.

Art is like singing, writing poems, and curiosity: It can very easily be ridiculed out of a child. Why is creativity so fragile? Still, people retain the wish to draw, the desire to make their surroundings pretty, even when they've given up on all the other realms of creativity. The bulky, brawny machismo might tell you, "Me? I have no eye for art. I can't tell a Michaelangelo from a soup can." And while he's telling you that, he's sweating in his yard, getting every last inch fed and trimmed and landscaped just so.

All the elementary teachers I've ever known, which is in the hundreds, have had one of two answers to the question. It's either, "Drawing is one of my most useful skills. I'm sure glad I can." — Or — "I sure wish I could."

Coloring books? Vote Yes!

Somewhere along the line, someone decided coloring books were bad. Not creative. Kids should create their own art; it's more meaningful. If you ever tried to draw an elephant for a child, or a helicopter, or Cookie Monster riding a horse, and you couldn't, or if *he* has tried to and couldn't, you understand the problem here. At the risk of being decreed an artistic and psychological heretic, here's why I *do* like coloring books.

— Identifying objects in outline form is a prerequisite to reading. Coloring books present them, in large, single-focus pictures: Find the car. What is this? (A train) What is Big Bird doing?

— The outlined forms in colorbooks are accurate. You can't tell a teeny child's circle from his square, and he absolutely *must* have accurate figures in order to read. Many, *many* kids fail to learn to read "on time" because they can't distinguish shapes. In a coloring book, a tot can see and *use* pictures months and years before he can make them himself.

— Adult criticism is minimized. When kids color, the harangues are limited to: *That's just scribbling. A tree isn't purple. Color the whole page before doing another. Don't use just one color. Don't eat the crayons.* And that's a lot less ragging than grownups do when the kid tries to draw his own.

— You can find colorbooks for particular interests and vocabulary development. Sesame Street characters, Beauty and the Beast or whatever the current rage; children's story classics; counting, letters, numbers; books of trucks, toys, people.

— Look. You can get a very nice, richly illustrated, durable hard-cover picture book of Animal Babies for $13.95. Or a very nice Animal Babies coloring book for 98 cents.

47

The gift of laughter

It's so important, psychologists have determined a minimum daily requirement. Twelve to fifteen titters and chuckles a day, and two to five bellylaughing guffaws.

The act of laughing changes your whole physiology, and that changes your whole outlook. Laughing releases chemicals which relax muscles, lower blood pressure, and counteract stress, anger, and fatigue. It is our best quick-fix attitude adjustment. It is a catalyst to comraderie: laughter bonds those who share it.

Everyone enjoys a good laugh ("They" always say it that way, as if there are good laughs and bad laughs), and from time to time, just about everyone pops a funny. But scientists fairly well agree that not everyone possesses the faculty to make people laugh, regularly and with consistency. Unlike the inborn sense of rhythm, a sense of humor is not necessarily universal to the species.

If a child begins to demonstrate a developing sense of humor, the adults in charge should make an effort to guide it. There's good humor and bad, tasteful and tacky, a high plane and a low, sophisticated and immature, intelligent and dumb.

Intelligent? Yes. A sense of humor is tightly tied to intelligence. And to a command of language.

I was in eighth grade when I learned three important lessons about being funny. Lesson One: Humor is a very personal thing. Everyone has his own perceptions about what's funny. I might think it's uproarious; you'll see it as inane, insulting, tacky, tasteless, or stupid. The second lesson is: Stupid gets you nowhere.

In the eighth grade I was kind of homely, and I hadn't yet learned to make passable music. So I needed something, and I found out I could make my classmates laugh. I figured they wouldn't understand anything very lofty, so to get the laughs I kept myself to the lowest level of corn.

One day my teacher returned a composition. He hadn't even bothered to grade it, but he had scrawled a red-lettered note across the top. "I'm sick and tired of this silliness," Mr. Olson wrote. There was more, but it was blurred and I couldn't see it, and I was so ashamed I pitched the paper before my eyes cleared to re-read it.

But Mr. Olson was right and I knew it, and I knew that without his bruising kick in the seat I could have been stuck in a pit of stupidity for who knows how many years. I should have told him so before I read his obituary.

That day I packed away the Abbott & Costello joke-alikes and moved to another plane. And, well, of course the kids got the higher drift — and that was Lesson Three: Don't underrate your audience.

Humor is both creative and intellectual. As with everything else in those realms, kids need examples and practice. Unfortunately there isn't a lot of mass-market stuff around that's what we could call exemplary humor. Look at prime time. Laugh tracks are tuned to sex and put-downs. Dan Fielding, Sam Malone, and Blanche Devareaux, the hustlers; and Roz, Carla, and Sophia, whose sole roles seem to be tossing out one-line insults. Nothing to do with any plot or story line, just character assassins whose payoff is fifteen quick recorded laughs per episode. The funnyness of home videos and hidden cameras is in pratfalls and embarrassment, and child brattiness.

A key to guiding your budding humorist is providing examples of the kind of mature, intelligent, thinking-persons' humor you wish your comedian to emulate. Here are examples of good examples.

— TELEVISION first, since it's generally the most readily accessible medium. There's *Sesame Street* (PBS). If your teen feels above ABC and 1-2-3, explain there's a lot of subtle, mature humor that's really aimed at big kids and adults, and tell him to watch for things that small children aren't likely to pick up.

There's *Faerie Tale Theatre* (PBS), which is most often a take-off on solemn, sober classics. Great opportunity to expose kids to parody. Ditto for Rocky and Bullwinkle's "Fractured Fairy Tales."

If your teenagers and college agers are up on current affairs, introduce them to the cerebral wit of *Mark Russell* and the *Capital Steps.* They assume their viewers are intelligent and informed, and they don't explain any of their parodies.

In a similar vein, many metro local channels carry homegrown parodies with names like *Almost Live* or *Friday Night.* The ones I've seen are higher off the streets than *Saturday Night.*

WKRP (syndicated): The original program was plain good all-ages comedy, with a marvelously textured blend of *sophisticana* and wacko. (But then, the original WKRP aired in an era when standards were cleaner.)

— FILM AND VID: *Raiders from Down Under* is full of humor and sight gags for big people. Ditto, *Bullwinkle* and pals.

Our standards of humor, as well as our standards of excellence in acting, staging, and photography, have changed dramatically over the years. Older youngsters can compare, analyze, and appreciate the differences. Subject matter and content have changed. In the olden days comedy was cleaner. And "zany," which, when used as a word promoting the comedy, meant "slapstick" — a.k.a. "dumb."

Some of the ancient comedies are worth searching for. *Victor Borge* made some half hour to hour-longs. Borge's humor was intelligent then and is now. Perhaps you can find him at your "vintage" video rental shop or your library. *Ma & Pa Kettle* (Marjorie Main & Percy Kilbride) had a rather lowbrow brand of humor, but it was funny, it was punny, and it was clean for its time, although today's Politically and Socially Correcters might squawk about some of its allusions and punnery.

Good for critical and analytical comparison: *Fred MacMurray, Hope & Crosby,* some of the standard bearers of their time. Maybe *Abbott & Costello* if you can stand them; your youngster could catch the word play and you could seize the opportunity to explain slapstick. And their "Who's On First" remains a classic.

Apparently everyone but me likes *Lucille Ball.* Even as a kid, I thought her dumb-dame klutziness was low-level witless; even before there was womyne's equality I thought her an insult to women. However, as a fair journalist, I recommend you introduce your older youngsters to her, if you can stand her yourself. (As an unfair journalist, I urge you to encourage your youngster to articulate why it is that Lucy's present-day fans are predominantly older persons, and then marvel together that the Gender Correct behaviorists haven't lynched Lucy.)

— PEN POWER: For serious study of humor, one needs to read it as well as watch it. (And be not misled: for a humorist, humor is serious. I said Serious and I said Study.)

What is funny about Dr. Seuss? *Why* is it funny? Why do children like it. and what is its appeal to adults? General rule: To sell humor to children, it must appeal to adults as well. Other studies in material ostensibly for little kids: *Peanuts* ; *Babar; The Elephant's Child.*

As soon as your kids can read them, have them study the prominent, role-model contemporary American humorists. Erma Bombeck. Garrison Keillor. Patrick McManus. Judith Viorst, Art Buchwald, Bill Cosby. Two sharply funny books about country life-and-animals, great family reading, are *Cattle Annie* (Ann Frey Cummins) and *Life in the Goat Lane* (Linda Fink). Both are marvellous studies in punnery, word play, intelligent humor; they even demonstrate the effective use of punctuation to enhance punch lines.

Unless one is determined to become a professional, you don't need to practice humor, in terms of going over and over it the way you practice jump shots or piano. Developing and refining wit, humor, and comedy happen from exposure, use, and growth, the way language is developed. It does matter *what* kinds of examples children are exposed to.

Wit and humor are high and complex intellectual activities. The witty person will always be sought out and popular — if the wit is channeled to enhance interpersonal relationships rather than degrade them. It involves values and judgments that can and must be taught. Emerging humor needs direction — and limits.

48

Of the creative person

By HEATHER SHIPE

Heather Shipe, a student at Hall-Dale High School, Hallowell, Maine, sees the creative-intuitive person as a wholly different personality than the logical-factual one. There is both poignance and defiance in her sense of being different.

To be creative is to be misunderstood, for the things we do are, at times, confusing to others. While they think of practical problems such as balancing a checkbook and homework, the creative mind dwells on issues such as finishing a story or beginning a painting.

To the unimaginative, the creative person seems to be in a daze. This is not true, for we see things others may miss. Fairies flying; the sun reflecting on puddles of water; viewing the world with eyes that miss nothing.

Everyone must march to his own drum, have his own personality. People seem to agree with this but then they alienate those whose personalities differ from theirs.

Such is the personality of a creative person. We see and believe in things others cannot or simply will not. For this our IQ is compared to that of a tic tac, but this is not true, for most creatives are highly intelligent. Intelligence and success need not only be an A+ on a math test; it can be a finished story or a beautiful painting. These too are achievements.

Achievements can come in any form. One achievement would be to accept creative persons the way we are. Where there is acceptance there is growth. Where there is growth — that is the ultimate achievement.

49

Imagination

Through his imagination, a child can create wondrous worlds and friends to put in them, sometimes a warmer world and more understanding friends than the ones of his reality. To four and five year olds, the world of his making may even be more real than the other one.

Not all people retain the imaginations that early-on appear. Persons whose thinking mode is wired to the purely concrete, those who more highly value facts and realism, the strictly scientific-method-minded, the very inhibited, the unstimulated, those who lack that particular creative aptitude or who simply don't enjoy that which is not real — those individuals may not retain a sense of the imaginary past the primary grades. To lack an imagination is not a dysfunction; it simply *is*.

A mother once told me regretfully that her daughter "doesn't seem to have any imagination." The child is bright — extraordinarily intelligent; and years ahead verbally. The thing is, she was barely two. It wasn't time yet for the imaginary to emerge. But it did, and on schedule. Don't look for qualities to appear before their time.

Imagination buds around age 3 and blooms by 4, says parenting columnist John Rosemund. Those who have long observed children, however, can affirm that kids under three take easily to pretending and imagining, particularly when they associate with youngsters two or three years older.

Imagination presents itself in so many forms it's . . . unimaginable! On highly sophisticated, intellectual, adult levels, man's imagination literally takes him to the galaxies. At one of those gatherings where some of the people knew some of the people and some didn't know anyone, I watched some 3, 4, and 5-year-olds at play. There was no sharp difference in sophistication, but there were differences in their modes.

"We're going to be princesses."

"No, I'm Mowgli and we're going to the Man Village. As "Mowgli" crossed a bridge on her way, she momentarily turned into the "Billiest Goat Gruff."

Mike, in contrast, needed to confirm their parameters. "We're just pretending, aren't we?"

The kids found some leaves which the princess declared would be butterflies. With three-year-old dramatics Mowgli said, "I'm going to cover mine with dirt and it'll grow *clear!* . . . *up!* . . . to the *SKY!* and we can CLIMB it!" Mike again confirmed, "These are really leaves, aren't they?"

As an everyday mode, the princess spends more of her time in physical action than she does imagining. Mowgli constantly plays roles, even assigns roles to the people around her. She lives in all sorts of other worlds and touches down on Earth merely to pass through and pick up more ideas to embellish. Mike, on the other hand, takes about one toe off the ground at a time.

Do you think Mowgli has problems with the real world, that she takes flight? — Or is she so glued-together that she can *afford* to soar off, knowing the world is secure, that it will be there, the way she left it?

Does it appear that Mike is so sure of his world that he doesn't need to imagine one? — Or is his reality so insecure that he's afraid to step away from it?

The fact is, you don't know; and from observing nothing of them but an hour, two hours, or a month of their play, you can't tell. The fact is, we all try to armchair analyze kids and very few of us have enough skill or information to do it. The fact is, both Mowgli and Mike are well-adjusted, bright, sociable little children who happen to have different degrees of imagination. More important, they have different modes of thinking and learning.

Mowgli simply has an active imagination. Perhaps she will be next generation's great American storyteller. With such extensive trips to Fantasyland, she appears to be a thinker in the random-abstract mode; but in fact she also operates in the concrete. Remember the child who learned about physical science with the rolling carrots? — She's the one!

Mike, in contrast, looks for science and form in almost everything he does. Before he was two, he could put a 24-piece puzzle together, the first time out of the box, faster than his dad. Mike loves stories, has a formidable rote memory and can repeat a Little Golden Book almost verbatim after a single reading; but when the story's over, it's over. He doesn't *live* the story the way Mowgli does.

Babies don't imagine. Infants think with their bodies, explains Thomas Armstrong of the National Parenting Center. They process and they think with their senses of sight, sound, taste, touch, and with movements. Toddlers and young children begin to think with their minds, but they mix fact and fantasy.

Logic begins to emerge between 5 and 6, says Armstrong, although at 4, Mike obviously realizes that leaves are not butterflies. The 5-year-old princess knows that, too; but she utilizes her logic to clarify that this is pretend.

Three-year-olds pretend because they are not yet logical. Six-year-olds use logic to explain that they are pretending.

Where little beginning-imaginers run into problems, explains Rosemund, is their inability to completely control the process. It gets away from them, and the bears and boogers they imagine themselves overcoming may overcome them. They turn into boogies under the bed and monsters in the closet.

Small children need names for things. Words put things into language and language makes things real. For 3 and 4-year-olds, Rosemund says, if there's a word for it, it's real. Trying to allay a little one's fear by telling him "monsters aren't real," then, is a contradiction.

So if the child's imagination runs amok and scares him, it's much more effective to help him slay his dragons than to try to convince him they never were.

As they begin to operate in the rational, logical mode, the majority of young people gradually put imaginary things away, like Wendy finally leaving the nursery. One phase gives way to another, the thought process that will assume lifetime dominance takes over. In fact, the teen and adult with a vivid imagination still intact is accused of "living in a fantasy world." Unfortunate terminology, because man's imagination put the tube in your living room, the popcorn in your microwave, and The Eagle Has Landed.

I expect that by the time he's 7 or 8, Mike will have abandoned the imaginary life, which he isn't living with much vavoom, anyway. He'll pursue the wonders of science with zesty enjoyment, unless the schools bludgeon the enthusiasm out of him.

Mowgli? Give up making up? I doubt it. But, then, neither did Dr. Seuss, Gene Roddenberry, nor Jim Hensen. Or Rudyard Kipling, either, who, after all, made up Mowgli.

> Imagination employs creativity, intellect, and language.
> Through imagination, a young child defines himself in his world. It reflects his mode of learning more than his psychological being.
> Adult imaginations solve problems, invent, and take us to the galaxies, figuratively and literally.

50

Immortality

I wanted to be remembered; to be, in some way, immortal.
I wrote my name on stalls and janitors painted them.
I wrote hundreds of stories and articles and people threw
away the books and magazines and papers, whether they read
them or not.
I composed dozens of pieces for my band, and the next
teacher disbanded the band and burned the music.
I taught hundreds of students who they were, and who
I was, and they graduated and forgot me.
On a sunny afternoon I answered the phone and heard
lusty squalling in the background. It was my son-in-law, calling
from the delivery room.
"Hi, Grandma," he said. "It's a girl."
I filled my cup and went out to the yard and looked up
at the sky and cried. At last, I had become immortal.

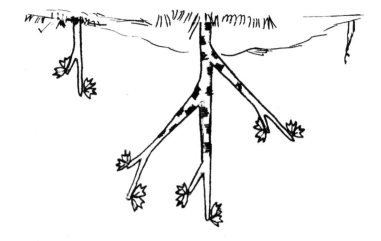